PRAISE FOR
BEYOND EXPECTATIONS

"I have known of Sydney Collier for quite a few years because of her equestrian accomplishments. Recently, I had the opportunity to meet through our mutual personal trainer in Wellington. I was always inspired by her cheerfulness and tenacity in her workouts. Because of this, I was honored and excited to be asked to be one of the first people to read an advance copy of her memoir *Beyond Expectations*.

"I was curious about her story and her journey towards the successes she has had. Once I started, it was hard to put down. What I learned was that her ability to overcome adversity and her power of positivity was indeed 'Beyond Expectations.' Anyone who reads this memoir will be entertained by and relate to her humor and occasional self-mockery. However, the real lesson to take away is that positive thinking and determination can lead to dreams coming true."

BEEZIE MADDEN
Olympic Gold Medalist, Two-Time Winner FEI World Cup Finals, Four-Time USEF Equestrian of the Year

"*Beyond Expectations* is a gripping memoir, simultaneously heartwarming and heart wrenching. Sydney takes us on 'her ride' from childhood dreams of being an Olympian to the most terrifying battle with a deadly diagnosis. Her story is one of incredible resilience and passion for her sport, as well as the amazing people and horses that helped save her life and forge her dreams!"

ROBERT DOVER
Six-Time Olympian, Former Technical Advisor US Dressage Team, Founder of the Equestrian Aid Foundation, and Author of *The Gates to Brilliance*

"I first met Sydney Collier at a Paralympic qualifier in Houston, Texas, when she was thirteen years old. I was immediately taken with her radiant and infectious positivity. She was like a breath of fresh air. I was utterly amazed…. It was the first time I truly understood what inspiration meant. Sydney is an immensely unique and special person, and the world can learn a lot from her."

COURTNEY KING-DYE
Olympian, Para Rider, Blogger, and Author

"In her moving memoir, Sydney Collier takes us along on the challenging journey that has been her life and her experience as an athlete and an equestrian. I felt I was right beside her through both her trials and her triumphs. I encourage everyone to get to know this determined young woman. Her book is hard to put down."

LENDON GRAY
Two-Time Olympian, Founder of Dressage4Kids Inc.,
Instructor, Coach, and Mentor

"Sydney Collier inspired us within the first two hours of meeting her. Her strength and courage, passion and dedication, happiness and positivity, and endless love toward horses has helped her achieve the goals she has wished and hoped for. She is an amazing young woman."

BEATRICE MARIENAU
FEI Dressage Competitor and Equestrian Sport Supporter
AND MICHAEL MARIENAU
Equestrian Sport Supporter

"For three years, I've known Sydney as she continues her mission of show ring excellence and empowering the next generation of riders. No one exudes more hope and optimism than she does. I get to see it weekly, and now she shares this message of optimism and the power of chasing down a dream with the world. The number of times I felt awe while reading through her memoir was too many to count. Sydney has the ability to connect with a wide audience. The messages that come out in the book are not just for people with a disability but for anyone who ever wanted to get more out of life. After reading Sydney's book, you will feel more motivated to chase down what you are after."

NICK FULLER CMPC
Sport Psychology Consultant

BEYOND EXPECTATIONS

An Extraordinary Equestrian Journey
from Deadly Diagnosis to the
Paralympic Games

SYDNEY COLLIER
US PARADRESSAGE TEAM MEMBER

and Heather Wallace

Foreword by Georgina Bloomberg

TRAFALGAR SQUARE
North Pomfret, Vermont

First published in 2024 by
Trafalgar Square Books
North Pomfret, Vermont 05053

Disclaimer of Liability
The author and publisher shall have neither liability nor responsibility to any person or entity with respect to any loss or damage caused or alleged to be caused directly or indirectly by the information contained in this book. While the book is as accurate as the author can make it, there may be errors, omissions, and inaccuracies.

Some names and identifying details have been changed to protect the privacy of individuals.

Trafalgar Square Books encourages the use of approved safety helmets in all equestrian sports and activities.

Trafalgar Square Books certifies that the content in this book was generated by a human expert on the subject, and the content was edited, fact-checked, and proofread by human publishing specialists with a lifetime of equestrian knowledge. TSB does not publish books generated by artificial intelligence (AI).

Library of Congress Cataloging-in-Publication Data
Names: Collier, Sydney, 1997- author. | Wallace, Heather (Equestrian),
　　author.
Title: Beyond expectations : a true story of growing up with a rare
　　disease, a deadly prognosis, and horses / Sydney Collier with Heather
　　Wallace.
Description: North Pomfret, Vermont : Trafalgar Square Books, 2024. |
　　Includes index.
Identifiers: LCCN 2023043638 (print) | LCCN 2023043639 (ebook) | ISBN
　　9781646011896 (paperback) | ISBN 9781646011902 (epub)
Subjects: LCSH: Collier, Sydney, 1997- | Collier, Sydney, 1997---Health. |
　　Dressage riders--United States--Biography. | Athletes with
　　disabilities--United States--Biography. | Women in horse sports--United
　　States--Biography. | Women athletes--United States--Biography. |
　　Horsemanship for people with disabilities. | Wyburn-Mason
　　syndrome--Patients--United States--Biography. | Paralympic Games (15th :
　　2016 : Rio de Janeiro, Brazil)--Anecdotes.
Classification: LCC SF309.482.C65 A3 2024　(print) | LCC SF309.482.C65
　　(ebook) | DDC 798.40092 [B]--dc23/eng/20240108
LC record available at https://lccn.loc.gov/2023043638
LC ebook record available at https://lccn.loc.gov/2023043639

Photographs courtesy of the author except where noted. *An effort was made to obtain a release from photographers whose images appear in this book. In some cases, however, the photographers were not known or could not be contacted. Should additional photographers be identified, they will be credited in future editions of this book.*

Interior and cover design by RM Didier
Typefaces: Merel

Printed in the United States of America

10 9 8 7 6 5 4 3 2 1

DEDICATION

I dedicate this book to my entire family.

When the entire deck appeared stacked against me,
you all believed in our ability to fight the odds together.

That means everything to me.

CONTENTS

FOREWORD

BY GEORGINA BLOOMBERG

The first time I met Sydney Collier I knew she was special. There was so much about her that was bold, in the best of ways, that she immediately captured my attention and made me want to know everything about her. From the obvious ways that met the eye—like the blueish purple color she had dyed her hair and her head-to-toe USA gear—to the large genuine smile that was constantly beaming across her face. In fact, her presence was so unique and captivating that I didn't notice she was in a wheelchair until we were a few minutes into a conversation. We talked about riding, our love of horses, and other animals, and about her already long list of accomplishments in the equestrian world.

I had never met a competitive para rider before Sydney. I had volunteered in therapeutic riding programs for years, and I had seen riders overcome incredible obstacles and challenges to be able to be on top of a horse, but this was something different that I knew nothing about. As a professional show jumper myself, I have experience with, and what I at least consider to be a strong understanding of the many layers of the equestrian world. But as I quickly discovered, there was a large, much more impressive and interesting layer that I didn't even know existed, and this unbelievably friendly and positive young woman sitting in front of me was inviting me in.

After our time together that day, I knew we would stay in touch and that my life would be better with Sydney in it. She had made me feel, in only a short time together, that I not only had gained a friend, but an inspiration. Not just an inspiration for my riding, but for my life. We did, in fact, stay in touch. I learned more and more about the para world every time we crossed paths, and my admiration for Sydney, in every way, grew and grew. But I still had no idea why she was in a wheelchair. It took years for me to even realize that I didn't know, and even then it wasn't until someone asked me, and it struck me that I had never really thought to learn about why.

There is something unexplainable about Sydney's ability to be vocal and passionate about para equestrian, completely open and comfortable with her story and who she is, and yet make whoever she is talking to forget that she is in a wheelchair. Over time I learned more and more about Sydney's story, and of course my respect and admiration of her grew as well. Here was a girl who had faced more challenges than I could imagine, and yet had accomplished much more than I ever had in my equestrian career. *And* managed to do it all with the most genuinely positive outlook toward everything in life, an enviable determination, and refusal to let anything get her down. She has a true pride in who she is and what she does. She is a fierce competitor, hard worker, and the proudest representative of Team USA I have ever met. But she is also an incredibly loyal friend, and the most thoughtful and kind young woman I know.

Somehow I knew when we met that Sydney would have an impact on my life. I was also quickly certain, as soon as my brain processed that this successful and obviously talented rider was in a wheelchair, that I would be impressed by her story and whatever it was that she had overcome to accomplish the things that most fully able bodied riders struggle to do. But what would leave the biggest impact on me, and what continues to do so every day since then, was not what she has won in the saddle, but the way she lives life and the person that she is. Her story is remarkable. Her challenges and what she, and her family, have been through unimaginable. And yes, for anyone who has ever ridden a horse, I am sure that after reading her story you will have the utmost respect for what she is able to do physically and her refusal to give up on her dreams. But what I hope you all get a sense of, and maybe even get to experience in person for yourselves one day if you are lucky enough to meet her, is that the smile on Sydney's face, her positivity and lust for making the most of everything, are all completely genuine. She never lets what she can't do have any affect on what she can do, and lets the latter fuel her enthusiasm for not just competing, but for life.

Yes, the day I met Sydney I knew she was special. But I didn't know that she would not only become my friend, but a role model for how I want to look at the world and live my life. Sydney is not just special, she truly is a hero.

Georgina Bloomberg
Professional Show Jumper and Philanthropist

PROLOGUE

The air was incredibly thick with anticipation—or maybe humidity. Perhaps it was a mixture of both. Everything that I had experienced in my life had led me to this moment, riding down the centerline of the arena at the Rio 2016 Paralympic Games. It was the culmination of years of hard work and drive to reach a challenging goal—this goal. And now, I was finally there.

It hadn't been a straight trajectory, but it was my journey.

This goal had often felt so big that I feared it might not happen. As cliché as it sounds, that emotional moment in Rio was a dream come true. I was proving to the entire world that I was good enough to compete at the highest level, even though I was not a typical dressage rider.

I worked my tail off to get there.

My partner that day was Western Rose, or "Rosie," for short. She was an Oldenburg mare, borrowed from my trainer. She was the horse chosen for me by the United States Para Dressage Team selectors because of her experience. She'd competed in the Paralympics previously with another rider and could show me the ropes. Rosie was steady but still required respect from her rider before she'd give 100 percent, so knowing I had succeeded in harnessing her talent to qualify for the Rio Team was surreal. I'd found a way to work through Rosie's strong opinions so, together, we could give our all out in the ring. For weeks, my trainer and I had worked to persuade the Para Dressage event organizers to allow me to "walk" the arena on foot before my competition. Because of my vision, or lack thereof, I needed time to familiarize myself with the ring to get my counts down. The organizers kept pushing back, saying it wasn't possible, until an hour before my ride, when they finally allowed me and my trainer to enter the arena. Talk about short notice!

I was already dressed in my full dressage competition gear, comprising white breeches, tall boots, and a blazer-style jacket with a white shirt underneath. The outfit was very steamy! The Brazilian sun reflected off the "sandbox" (a nickname dressage riders commonly use for the arena), making it even hotter and straining my good eye with its glare. I walked into the ring on foot, my trainer beside me, because the sand was too deep for the scooter I usually sit in to run. As a result, we had to move at an excruciatingly slow pace so I wouldn't trip, all while knowing that we had precious little time before the competition began. I had never wished to be carried on the back of a horse more in my life! I limped along, exhausted, through the arena that seemed to grow larger with each step I took forward.

We certainly hadn't expected this before my Paralympic debut, but my trainer and I laughed and went with it. What else could we do? While it threw off our preparatory timing a bit, it was a necessary step for me to be able to ride my test successfully.

The warm-up went very well, all things considered. We focused on transitions to get Rosie supple in the mouth and accepting my one-handed rein with forward energy. It went by quickly (which wasn't necessarily a bad thing), and then, suddenly, it was my turn to enter the arena, this time on Rosie, and I didn't have time to think about being nervous or too excited.

Rosie and I were so attuned to each other during that test, nothing else mattered. We could have been anywhere, in any ring, and we would have communicated as one entity. My ride felt like slow motion as the crowd roared, and their excitement filled me. The heat of the sun blazing down on us, making the arena glow brighter, my horse moving underneath me, and the exhilarating sound of the spectators cheering us on was like a dream. In fact, it was better than all the dreams I'd had in the past five years, because this was real.

Riding down the centerline that afternoon in Brazil was a defining moment in my life. All the challenges I had faced could have meant taking a different road. Yet, in some ways, those challenges were why I was able to experience something few people in life do—the thrill of competing for your country against the best athletes in the world. Like a building block, each challenge in my life had brought me higher, lifting me to this pinnacle. On the cusp of completing a goal that had once seemed impossible while lying in my hospital bed as a young child, I felt joy in the reward for hard work, thankful for the forces known as serendipity, and immense gratitude for the horses who lent me their legs when mine had an agenda of their own. These three things were the foundations of this defining moment.

I'm excited to share my story with you.

ORIGIN STORY

was told at seven years old I wasn't supposed to be alive.

It sounds dramatic, but it's the truth.

At that age, the ramifications of that one doctor's appointment were unfathomable. It focused me on "more important things," like playing with my friends and riding horses. It irrevocably changed the lives of every member of my family. I was "built differently," and in the end, that would mean my life, more than others, had a time limit.

Thanksgiving 1997 brought something new for my family to be thankful for...me! My mother had invited everyone to dinner—her parents, my dad's parents, my uncles. She was so excited to host. Then her water broke, and she ended up in the hospital for the entire holiday.

The first few hours of labor were peaceful, apparently. My father is a psychologist, and he'd had Mom take birth hypnosis classes in preparation for my delivery. She doesn't remember the first five hours to this day. It was only when a nurse questioned her and told her hypnosis didn't work that she started feeling the contractions, which, of course, made her just a little upset! It's funny how instilling a sliver of doubt can unravel months of hard work and preparation.

I wasn't ready to come out. After twenty-eight hours of labor, my mom needed a C-section. I've been a pain in her butt ever since. But my mom loves to say that everyone remarked on my beautiful blue eyes from the moment I was born. Ironically, they turned out to be what led to my diagnosis years later.

My childhood was typical in the best of ways. I could even say it was picture perfect. My family lived in the suburbs of Illinois where I was surrounded by kids my age, as my mom and the other women in the neighborhood had all had babies around the same time. I got a lot of attention, especially since I was my parents' first child, and after my two brothers were born, the only girl.

I went to school and had playdates with friends. I vividly remember celebrating warm summer days, running through sprinklers. My younger brothers and I did all the things that children do: joking, fighting, and making core memories. My mom was a superwoman, balancing our schedules and seemingly never intimidated by having three children, plus all our pets! She gave us everything we needed to thrive. When I think back to those early days of my childhood, I can still feel the sunshine on my skin as I ran with my brothers, laughing wildly at some antic or another.

Life was good.

I found my passion early in life. I was utterly obsessed with four-legged animals. "Rideable" bouncy horses were a favorite toy of mine. I never wanted the Bratz doll or the Barbie; I enjoyed playing with Breyer model horses. Whenever my mother went grocery shopping, I begged to ride on the motorized horse outside the storefront. I was on a pony ride whenever the opportunity struck. Horses became a steady undercurrent in my life.

Sometimes things feel meant to be.

My mom helped plant the seeds that took my interest in horses from

  BEYOND EXPECTATIONS

playing with toys to becoming an equestrian. I tried every type of sport as a kid. Basketball wasn't a good fit. I've always been short. And I was out on the field, picking dandelions, daydreaming in my own little world, during soccer practice. My mom would say, "Soccer is pretty good, but how about those horses?" She had grown up with horses herself, cleaning stalls in exchange for riding time. Eventually, she had earned her own horse, Top of the Hill Wild Music, and I loved hearing stories about her times with him. He sounded like a horse no one else wanted, but Mom had loved him exactly as he was, no holds barred. I longed for a relationship like that with a horse.

When I asked for riding lessons, my mom was so elated she signed me up the next day at a local barn. I was seven years old.

After I walked into a barn for the first time, I never looked back. It instantly felt like a second home to me: the sounds of hay being chewed, tails whipping flies, and little sneezes and nickers of contentment. The smell of horses, and yes, manure, was inviting. When I entered the barn and saw the horses all lined up in their stalls, it felt like they were waiting for me to arrive. I breathed it all in and felt a sense of "rightness," knowing I was where I belonged. I practically bounced into the arena in my excitement, instantly craving a ride on the biggest, fanciest horses. It never occurred to me I wouldn't immediately get on them! When my first instructor took me to the cross-ties and introduced me to my lesson partner, I admitted some disappointment aloud—instead of the Barbie Dream Horse, a small, fluffy pony waited for me. Ponies were for little kids. I wanted to ride the big ones.

Of course, my riding instructor knew better than I did, and despite my initial feelings, the fluffy pony turned out to be incredible! Macy was approximately thirty-one years old, and the safest choice for a child just starting out. Her ears were gigantic. To this day, I can clearly see them standing straight up, with tufts of hair coming out of them, like a stuffed animal. No one knew what breed Macy was, but the ears made us joke that she must have some donkey in her! Bouncy horses and pony rides may have jumpstarted my passion, but little Macy solidified it. She could hang with the big horses despite her size—and even show them up! At one show jumping rally where Macy and I competed, we took home first prize with a stunning twenty-six-second jump-off, while all the "fancy" horses completed the jump-off in forty-five seconds or more!

Macy was the perfect example of small but mighty, and she never quit. What she lacked in size she more than made up for in heart. I couldn't help but fall in love with her. And I made it a habit to never underestimate a horse based on appearance after that. It took me a lot longer to appreciate that the same rule applies to people, as well. Looks can be and are deceiving.

Macy and I, it would turn out, would have a lot in common.

One of my fondest memories of my time with Macy is playing gymkhana games with a flag and barrel. The first time we tried, no one had told me she used to be a "gaming pony." I found out quickly! We approached the first barrel at a decent, rhythmic canter, but once I grabbed the flag, she made a beeline for the next barrel, rocketing down the line as fast as her little legs could carry us. I remember thinking, *I thought she was old!* I dropped the flag and held on for dear life, not out of fear but sheer joy. The feeling of the wind in my face and the pony pumping her legs under me was freedom! We spoke each other's language, and we both loved speed.

Pony Club became a massive part of my growing knowledge of horses. My closest barn friends joined Pony Club with me. My mom and another mom were co-leaders of our club, and we had weekly meetings at one of our homes, all the while learning more and more about horses and developing closer friendships that would last a lifetime.

As a Pony Club leader, my mom was the queen of organization! Everything had a "Cedar Ridge Pony Club" label, and we all had our own first aid and safety kits. When there was a craft project, you bet my mom oversaw it! Our Pony Club traveled to compete in nearby horse knowledge "quiz rallies" and (my favorite!) show jumping rallies. Macy was my partner for all these glorious Pony Club activities. To this day, I attribute much of my knowledge of proper horse management, the horse's anatomy, and different kinds of tack to my time in Pony Club. Through it, I learned the basics of my passion. The camaraderie I built with my barnmates was unlike anything I had ever experienced before. There's nothing like a shared love for horses to unite people!

Soon after, I began to dream that one day I would qualify to compete on the United States Equestrian Team in three-day eventing at the Olympics. I was a total daredevil, always wanting bigger jumps and faster speeds. I never worried about my safety.

And then, everything changed.

EVERYTHING CHANGES

When I was born, my grandma told my mother that I had an old soul she could see through my clear, blue eyes. Even now, everyone comments on how bright and striking my eyes are. Perhaps it's an example of how ironic the world has been in my experience that my eyes would be the reason my condition was discovered.

Like most children, my earliest years are a blur of snapshot-like moments and events. I recall happy times with my parents and brothers, family vacations, and riding horses at the nearby barn.

It all changed because I wanted to wear glasses.

My second-grade teacher had noticed I struggled to see the board and recommended I sit at the front of the class and get an eye exam. I thought visiting the ophthalmologist was incredibly exciting. Glasses were just the coolest to me, and it had been a dream of mine to own a pair of my own. I imagine the visit was fairly routine for my eye doctor, at the beginning. After all, plenty of children struggle with their vision and need glasses to help them see better. However, I have never done anything halfway and probably gave her a mild heart attack! At the very least, I am the patient she will never forget.

You see, during my "routine" eye exam, the doctor looked into my right eye and saw an AVM—that stands for arteriovenous malformation, which is often described as "a tangle of blood vessels that irregularly connects arteries and veins, disrupting blood flow and oxygen circulation."

The blood drained from my doctor's face, turning her sheet white. It's funny how, even though I was so young at the time, I still remember the moment vividly, as she said, "I don't know if I should call an ambulance, send you to the hospital, or what I should do. I never thought I would see this case in my entire career, let alone my entire life."

I'm sure my parents took me to the opthamologist that day, thinking I would probably need glasses, and we'd move on with our lives. They couldn't have been more wrong. Our entire "normal" world's foundation shattered at that moment.

My parents were fantastic—as composed as they could be, given the situation. They didn't panic overtly, wanting to keep me calm, and took me straight to the hospital on the ophthalmologist's recommendation to get an MRI to confirm what she believed she had seen during my exam. Doctors recommended anesthesia for the MRI because of my young age. A nurse came in to prep me, and as required by law, informed my parents of all the potential complications from sedation. Imagine being seven years old, confused about why you're suddenly in the hospital (without the glasses you dreamed of, I might add), and overhearing all the risks of "THE TEST." I wondered if I would die. I cried, begging my parents to allow me to have the MRI without anesthesia. I promised I could lie entirely still, "like a mummy," and my parents went along with my request. They knew I was determined and capable. (Privately, my parents might have used the word "stubborn"—but only as a compliment, of course!)

I just wanted to come out of the MRI machine alive. It scared the living crap out of me! It was enormous and loud, and the test went on for what seemed like an eternity as I wondered if I was going to live or die.

The MRI told us it was true: I had an AVM behind my right eye and another one deep in my brain. I also now had a preliminary diagnosis: Wyburn-Mason syndrome. So, in fact, I very well might die.

An AVM is like a tumor with high blood flow, as the veins and the arteries don't separate via the usual network of tiny blood vessels (capillaries) that normally help control blood flow. It looks like a bag of worms on an MRI. The National Organization for Rare Disorders (NORD) explains that "without the capillaries, there can be damage to the walls of the arteries and veins, causing abnormal and high blood flow and leakage." This means there is a catastrophic risk of bleeds and stroke, which can lead to death.

Wyburn-Mason syndrome is a rare, nonhereditary, congenital disorder. Affected individuals have AVMs like mine, usually found in the eyes and brain. Fewer than 100 cases of Wyburn-Mason syndrome have been reported, according to the National Institute of Health. Most diagnoses have been confirmed by pathologists in infants after death.

It was a miracle I had even lived to see seven years. It had never happened with a known Wyburn-Mason case before.

My parents were understandably terrified. I had a ticking time bomb in my head. They were living their own personal nightmare.

When we discussed treatment options, the doctor straightforwardly said, "Take her home and pray she doesn't die of a massive bleed. That's all you can do."

My mom, rightfully so, confronted him: "If this was your own kid, would you be okay with a doctor telling you that?"

We left immediately, and my mom began tirelessly combing the internet, searching for weeks for any treatment possibility. She found only two Wyburn-Mason specialists in the world. Luckily, one of them was Stanford Medical Center in California, which wasn't impossible to reach from our home in Illinois. The other was in Switzerland and not an option. Mom reached out at once for help, and Stanford Medical Center returned her call. They told her that while they had successfully treated AVMs previously, they had never dealt with those associated with Wyburn-Mason, and they had only worked with adult patients. I would be their first pediatric case—but they agreed to a consult.

As a child, I didn't understand the true ramifications of the ophthalmologist finding the AVMs. While I might have feared "dying," I was too young to really understand my mortality, and thankfully, my parents put on a brave face, focusing on solutions, not the diagnosis. They didn't let me see their own fear.

My mind was not on my health through the period of my initial diagnosis and treatment planning. It singularly focused on any time I could spend with horses. My passion for the animals and riding carried me through. I was happy if I could still ride. Thank God my parents were even-keeled. They never held me back or kept me from the barn. I had a slight lack of coordination and vision issues, but I still was overtly able-bodied at that point. Later in my childhood, when I was pursuing eventing, I had a rotational fall off a bank. Both my horse and I were okay, but I got a a gnarly concussion. We ended up in the hospital because of the concussion, but Mom and Dad still never held me back from setting big goals or tried wrapping me in bubble wrap. My brothers, who are able-bodied "easy keepers," and I were always treated the same. That was the biggest thing for me. My mom and dad knew horses were keeping me fighting to live, so they never limited me and what I could try to do when many other parents may have. I'm sure I often made their blood pressure spike, though, and that worry was ever-present.

After an initial consult, we traveled back and forth to California, and I was pulled out of school for weeks at a time and away from my brothers, whose lives my parents tried to keep as normal and calm as possible. Because they were younger than me, they understood even less about what was happening. Along with horses, my brothers helped keep a sense of normalcy in our life. Despite my diagnosis, they never treated me differently and only saw me for me. My mom and dad held it all on their shoulders. The weight must have been unbearable. To this day, they won't admit how hard it must have been for them. They made so many sacrifices for my treatment—and for my equestrian dreams to come true. It was an enormous commitment.

It would have been so easy to get lost in the darkness. Everything was clearly not sunshine and roses. My mind spun when doctors told me the first course of my treatment would include CyberKnife radiation. I could only imagine what the room where THAT took place would look like! I envisioned cyborg-type knives, dancing around my head—honestly, that's what I pictured! In reality, CyberKnife is an advanced form of radiosurgery that delivers high doses of targeted radiation to destroy tumors or lesions within the body. It sounds scary, but is noninvasive and should be painless.

Later, when I began experiencing more symptoms, including a severe burning at the bottom of my left foot, it meant we had to think about accelerating treatment. Not long after, I had a migraine for an entire year. I was miserable all the time. Well, almost always. The only thing that relieved the constant pain was my time in the saddle. Miraculously, my symptoms would ease when I rode horses—for a short time, I would feel normal again.

My family never ignored the low points, but I'm lucky to have parents that focus on the positive, letting "bad things" sit in the past. I think the whole "make lemonade out of lemons" cliché is their motto! My life would have been a lot different if we hadn't had that perspective. I wouldn't have accomplished anything like what I have if I'd taken the opposite approach. They nurtured my optimism and led by example.

Life has a funny way of turning the tables on you when you least expect it. I can't imagine any parent reacting well to the news that their child would likely die, and that it would happen suddenly. My diagnosis flipped my parents' entire world upside down; one appointment, and their lives were forever changed. Everything they knew, out the window. Suddenly, there was a countdown clock, hovering over our family.

How long did I have to live?

DEADLY DIAGNOSIS

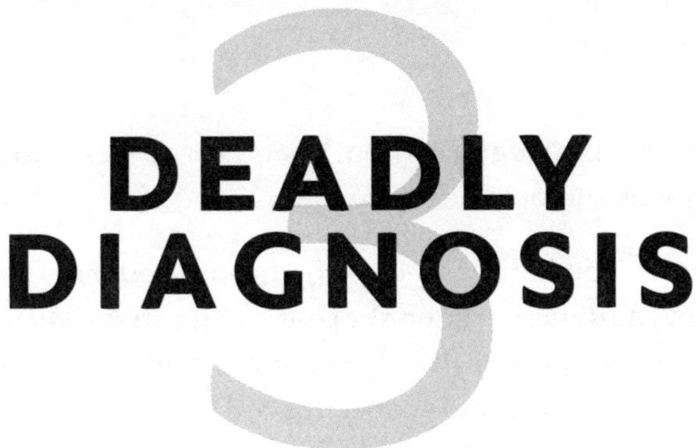

yburn-Mason syndrome is actually very complex to understand. It is important to categorize it as a (congenital) birth defect, not a disease. A baby is born with AVMs, which occur when the baby develops in utero. Wyburn-Mason is such a rare defect that very little information is available on the subject. It is usually diagnosed in infants only after they have died of a massive brain bleed.

Life expectancy is incredibly low.

It shocked my doctors to see a case in their lifetime; I was a unicorn for medical personnel!

It is funny how something as simple as blurred vision changed the course of my life forever.

Because AVMs are so fragile and mine were in such complex-to-treat areas, it took a specialist hospital to begin treatment. I began CyberKnife radiation at eight years old. CyberKnife radiation uses gamma rays that are finely tuned and exact, much more so than what many of us know as cancer radiation. However, the radiation is so precise, there is no room for error, or it could be catastrophic.

The goal was to reduce the size of some of my blood vessels. We were told it would take between six months and three years to see if it had any effect. It was the only hope we had.

I had to wear a special mask during the procedure. I looked like a movie villain. Medical personnel created the mask with mesh they dipped in warm water and then formed over my face while I was in a CT (computed tomography) scan. I prayed I wouldn't have to sneeze! It was incredibly itchy, and it did NOT smell like daisies! It was a true test of willpower to sit for this part of the process.

Then the medical staff strapped me onto a hard, flat slab. I always brought my "blankie," which was covered in horses, for the nurses to put over me for comfort while I was cinched tightly, as if I were Hannibal Lecter, threatening to eat the doctors for a tasty snack. I felt like a science experiment.

Each CyberKnife session was about thirty minutes. The plastic was incredibly pungent, and I had to be awake and absolutely still for the duration. I am so grateful I don't have lasting PTSD from the experience! My first treatment, with frequent sessions, took approximately one month. It was an experimental procedure to use the radiation on my AVMs. Not to brag, but I'm kind of famous in medical journals.

In addition, my family also explored other limited treatment options that involved angiograms (imaging that showed how well blood was flowing through my blood vessels) and steroids. I learned quickly how much I despised the latter. Steroids became the bane of my existence, and I still will avoid them to this day when given the opportunity. If I was being dramatic, I would say I hate them "with the fire of a thousand suns"—but even that wouldn't do it justice. Steroids reduced the swelling in my brain, which could provide some necessary relief; however, the swelling increased throughout the rest of my body. The side effects were terrible. Even when, years later, I had a year-long migraine, I still refused the doctor's offer to use steroids to ease my pain.

 BEYOND EXPECTATIONS

Sitting in the hospital wasn't fun, but as time went by, it became necessary. Luckily, we made it a family experience. My parents and brothers, Alex and Simon, would come with me, and we would go sightseeing and have "mini-vacations" after my treatment sessions. The Redwood forests, the Pacific coastline, the mountains—we saw them all. Because of this, our travels to California were always love- and adventure-filled times, and I never focused on the medical aspect. On one trip, after I received clearance and was released from the hospital, I begged (rather annoyingly) to go to the beach. I wore my family down, and they finally agreed. I had just undergone a femoral angiogram to look for abnormalities in the blood vessels in my brain. No big deal, right?

We drove along a two-lane road up the mountain, with a cliff on one side. Suddenly, I became sick to my stomach. We pulled off into a little parking area. I threw open the door and began to projectile vomit from the side of the car with my nose pouring blood. When I was done, I wiped my nose, took a deep breath, and looked up to see a hippie couple in a camper van watching the entire horrible scene. I can't even imagine what they thought was happening. But they smiled at us and laughed, saying, "Ah, we have all been there, right?"

After I finished losing the contents of my stomach and cleaned myself up, we got back on the road and eventually spent the day at the beach as if the blood and vomit had never happened.

My family had a remarkable ability to clearly focus on the good times we had together, even when I am sure they were stressed beyond measure or reason. My treatments at Stanford Medical Center were a Hail Mary, and we didn't even know if everything we were enduring would ever be successful. Still, I never glimpsed the fear and weariness they must have felt. Looking back, I realize just how much they needed some normalcy in those days, too. One example was a particular parental joke that backfired.

The weather was always beautiful in California. To my mom and dad's chagrin, I hated driving with the windows open in the car. The wind effect created a sensory overload for me and I'd vocally complain—relentlessly. On one trip, my brothers stayed at home with my grandparents, and desperate for the fresh air, my mom and dad rolled down every single window in the car. I was distraught. But when I protested, they pointed out visible paths on the mountains on either side of the road and said, "Syd, whenever we see paths like that, the rental car company made us agree to roll down the windows completely because those paths mean there are mountain lions. The mountain lions need to jump directly through the car to get to the other side of the road. If we shut the windows, they'll dent it and cause damage."

At first, I stuck to my guns, not one to be gullible, and still disturbed by the excess airflow. But my parents' insistence that there were mountain lions steadily wore my confidence down as we drove, and I noticed more and more of these paths. I begged them to roll the windows up, and they continued to say they couldn't because then the mountain lions wouldn't be able to jump through. Sure enough, my nerves shredded, and I broke down sobbing. I don't think my parents expected me to get so rattled by their joke; unfortunately, instead of lightening the mood and making me laugh, it overwhelmed me.

While there was always a medical undercurrent on our trips, our times together as a family are the memories that really stick with me. My parents, brothers, and doctors never limited me, and it's part of why I am so strong today. They never treated me like I was different or had to be bubble-wrapped. I wasn't a specimen. I was always a person to them first.

One thing I could never pass up was a ride on a roller coaster. I have always been a daredevil, searching for the adrenaline rush and living in the moment—it's one of the reasons eventing and jumping cross-country appealed to me. While usually all for my sense of adventure, my mom did hesitate at the idea of sending me off on roller coasters and said, "Absolutely not without your doctor's approval."

Sometimes it is hard to read doctors. They can have wonderful poker faces. But when we asked my doctor at our next appointment if

I could go to the Six Flags theme park, he looked at me, then at my parents, and just said, "You let her ride thousand-pound animals for fun. I don't see why she couldn't go to an amusement park."

Score!

My doctor recommended a little Dramamine, but otherwise, he said I didn't have any limitations at the theme park. He, and my other doctors, too, knew how much horses and living life to the fullest kept me strong and diverted focus from my medical issues. Maintaining a sense of fun and normalcy helped me to concentrate on healing and gave me something to look forward to after the hospital stays.

For my eighth birthday, following my diagnosis, my parents, uncles, and grandparents decided we should take a family trip to Walt Disney World in Orlando, Florida. I was obsessed with Disney princesses at the time, especially Cinderella. When they told me we were going, I was so excited I couldn't even put how I was feeling into words! But inside I was buzzing with anticipation—I was going to get to meet real-life princesses and princes! My birthday dinner included a "meet and greet" with Cinderella herself! I was over the moon.

My brother Alex was six years old at the time, and Simon was only four. They weren't old enough to go on many of the rides, and neither were big fans of standing in lines for hours, waiting to get on the rides, as you must at Disney World. This made the trip challenging at some points.

When we went to Universal Studios, there was a "virtual experience ride" straight out of the movie *Twister*, which was an action-adventure film about storm chasers that starred Bill Paxton and Helen Hunt. I remember so vividly being excited that it was one of the few rides my entire family could go on together. But as the virtual tornado started to swirl, and a cow appeared to take flight and get sucked into it, just like in the movie, I heard the loudest shriek I have ever heard—to this day. The bone-chilling sound was little Alex, having an existential crisis about the cow. My dad couldn't get him out of the ride quickly enough! Simon and I were fine, though. Alex has always been a bit more reserved, whereas Simon and I have more bull-in-the-china-shop personalities and don't get scared by much.

◇ ◇ ◇

Few of us understand how pivotal individual moments can be be in our lives. My teacher recommending I get glasses began the unravelling of a series of events: the eye doctor, the emergency room...a devastating diagnosis.

Still, even as larger forces seemed to take control of our lives, I remained hyper-focused on one thing—that first thing that I had dreamed about: getting a pair of excellent glasses. Would they help improve my vision? No. Not with my diagnosis. But I was determined to have them, anyway. I still remember exactly what my first glasses looked like. They were glorious purple square-frames with polka dots. To top it off, I had purple transition lenses to up my cool factor all the way.

Whenever I do something, it is with gusto.

Because I achieved my goal, I still felt I walked away from the emergency room a winner. Even when I was sharing the news of my diagnosis with my friends at school, I joked, "Guys, I am going to be in the *Guinness Book of World Records* because I'M THE FIRST KID TO EVER GET TREATED FOR WYBURN-MASON SYNDROME!"

The ultimate positive outlook!

I have never seen my diagnosis as something that has alienated me from others. With the help of my family, I have seen it as something that makes me more unique and more me.

It is so important to celebrate our uniqueness—our differences. This is a belief that has guided my entire life.

BRIDGING THE GAP

Until I was eight years old, I "catch rode" other people's horses and ponies every day. No matter what happened at school or with the doctors, the barn and time with horses made everything okay.

DCA Muscany Lane was a pinto Arabian with a heart of gold. My family bought her for me so I could pursue the sport of eventing, which I loved, but "Lacey" was not a fan of cross-country jumping. She preferred show jumping and flatwork, which both occurred in a riding arena instead of out in the open fields or woods. But despite her dislike of cross-country, Lacey taught me how to truly love a horse. Her eyes were so kind, and I always knew she understood how the long hours in treatment, the endless waiting rooms, and all the boring and upsetting stuff just reset and lifted away when I was with her.

I grew up in Michigan, went to a popular local barn, and made many friends there, with horses as our shared passion. I needed the respite, the time away from the stress of my life. Horses were an oasis of calm and consistency in a very scary world.

I just wanted to be a regular kid, but that wasn't in the cards for me.

More symptoms began showing up after my first course of CyberKnife radiation. My brain was reshaping itself, and the expectation was always that my condition would likely advance, and that complications and side effects from my treatments might occur. Still, it was almost impossible to prepare for the fallout.

I was nine, sitting in my classroom at school, when suddenly my right eye went completely black. Immediate, complete darkness. It was terrifying, like someone shut off the lights, but only on one side. It caused severe disorientation.

Not even two years before, my vision problems that led to my initial diagnosis had started at school; now, here I was again in the same situation. I stayed to the end of the school day and then went home to tell my parents that in a split second—or dare I say, "in the blink of an eye"—I had lost all sight from my right eye.

In addition, I was experiencing a burning sensation in my left foot, like I was walking over hot coals, especially when I applied pressure. My riding instructor's call for "heels down" created intense burning and pain from the pressure in the stirrup that brought involuntary tears to my eyes. Subtle coordination issues accompanied the new unevenness in my body from the left-to-right-side foot discomfort and lack of vision. Riding a bike became difficult, and I would tilt, falling to one side with no idea why.

Then, around age ten, I got a headache. It came on like any other, and I was determined to push through it to go to school. My mother was always a stickler about the rule that if I didn't feel well enough to go to school, I certainly wasn't feeling well enough to go to the barn later in the day. She knew how to get me to power through. It certainly prevented me from complaining about little things!

Except this headache progressed to the point where I couldn't leave my room. The pain was debilitating, and even small sounds hurt. My senses were in overdrive, and I couldn't function. My mother put up full blackout shades, and my bedroom became a kind of sensory-deprivation chamber. Still, the pain didn't lessen. I could barely eat. It was the most pain I've ever been in my life. I wondered if it was the AVMs or a side effect of the radiation. Nothing eased the chronic pain.

Nothing, that is, except one thing, and one thing only. The pain was so extreme that it completely incapacitated me, with a single exception.

Riding horses.

If I could power through standing up without vomiting, getting dressed, and managing the car ride to get to the barn to ride Lacey, I would feel slightly better for a short while. It never lasted. I still don't know why riding helped. The doctors couldn't explain it. There was no medical or rational explanation. But riding was the only thing that got me on my feet and kept me going.

The head pain was so intense I was overprescribed medication in an attempt to offer me some relief. Morphine, oxycodone, and hydromorphone are just a few of the highly addictive painkillers doctors put me on—potent narcotics for anyone, much less a young girl. But they didn't help for long. It got so bad that I was taking pills every hour, and the pain was *still* severe. The scenario was incredibly unhealthy, and the poison I was dumping into my body didn't even numb the pain.

Desperate, my parents reached out to my California doctors, and I returned to Stanford for another assessment.

While in the Stanford pediatric ward, doctors tried everything, taking an integrative approach from Western and Eastern medicine that included, among other things, a hydromorphone drip, mindfulness, meditation, acupuncture, and spinal taps. Nothing helped. There is a photo of me sitting outside on the roof of the building, surrounded by the Center's gorgeous California campus, and I'm slumped over with immense circles under my eyes (the very photo featured in the background on the cover of this book). I looked, and felt, like a drug addict—not a feeling I'd ever expected to know at the ripe old age of ten.

We left California because I needed to get back to my horse, my only source of relief, and if there was no improvement in my pain with the doctors' treatment, what was the point of waiting?

Once home, my parents had to figure out how to detoxify my system from all the narcotics we had been trying. I went through withdrawal. It's mind-blowing that I was even in that situation at ten years old. I felt defeated and depressed. It was a truly dark period in my life.

The only light was Lacey. Spending time in the saddle with her gave me respite from the excruciating pain.

The migraine lasted an entire year, and then it slowly tapered off, until one day, it disappeared as suddenly as it had begun. I don't know if the inflammation from the radiation treatment abated or if my body just became used to it.

In a devastating blow to my family and doctors, who hoped we were in for a celebration of "blood flow shrinkage" and perhaps even signs of a cure, another exploratory angiogram found out that my CyberKnife treatment had had no effect on my AVMs. Nothing we'd tried had been successful.

The doctors changed tactics, and, believing I was a suitable candidate, recommended a high-risk brain surgery as my next treatment option. It was an arthroscopic surgery that used *embolization*—a procedure that the National Cancer Institute describes as using "particles, such as tiny gelatin sponges or beads, to block a blood vessel"—and my family agreed to try. The surgeons operated through my femoral artery, using an injectable dye to trace the neural pathways up to the brain. After that, they injected a special glue to close off some of the blood flow to the AVMs.

The surgery was textbook, and everyone was happy with the results—especially my neurosurgeons.

Or so they thought.

On the way from the operating room to the pediatric ICU, I had my first massive stroke at eleven years old.

As I woke up from sedation, my left side felt droopy. I remember my mother telling the ICU nurse something was wrong, but the nurse disagreed and argued that I was the same as when I came in. My mother was correct—she was noticing the symptoms of a stroke. To this day, I wonder if my mom feels that if she could only have convinced the ICU nurse that something was wrong sooner, perhaps the effects of the stroke wouldn't have been so severe.

There are many what-ifs, especially with Wyburn-Mason syndrome and the high-risk procedures that can go along with treatments. I was an experiment in many ways for medical personnel.

There aren't many photos or videos of our experiences as a family during this time. I asked my mother why that was the case, because a lot of that period seems like a blur to me, and I don't know whether that blurry memory is the result of all the medication I was on, the trauma I was experiencing, or the fact I was so young. My mother replied that my family had to see a lot of death during that period.

It was a dark time for them, managing my medical treatments, taking care of my brothers, and spending so many days and nights in the hospital, worrying about me. As hard as it was for me to experience, my parents had it just as bad.

After my stroke, I was transferred to an in-patient rehabilitation center in California. I was the youngest one in the stroke ward—always the overachiever! I do like to be daring and different. I stayed in the in-patient facility, my parents alternating nights spent on the uncomfortable rehab "recliner" (if you could even call it that). The parent who didn't stay with me slept in the rental house with my grandparents, who were visiting to try to help lessen the stress and support our family.

Nights with my dad were my personal favorite. There were a lot of fast-food restaurants in the area, and my dad and I took full advantage. Hospital food is usually terrible, but this rehabilitation facility was shockingly lacking in even basic culinary skills. Without me even asking, my dad would sneak us takeout treats to enjoy together after a long day of physical and occupational therapy, plus any other therapy you could imagine. He would go for a jog every night he spent with me, then bring us back an Oreo McFlurry to share. It was always the highlight of my dark day. The happy moments that were interspersed with so much trauma are what I remember. That's what I choose to focus on when thinking back to that time of my life.

It was hard not having the horses nearby and being so far from the rest of my family. The separation drove me harder to improve and recover so I could return home. After two months, my rehabilitation was deemed successful. I could still use my left hand and needed only an AFO (ankle-foot orthosis) brace on my left leg to supply support and stability but still allow me to walk easily.

It was time to go home and prepare for seventh grade. I was really looking forward to getting back to some sense of my form of normalcy! Going to school and the barn was a routine I craved because my life had been full of chaos, doctors' visits, and pain. "Normal" for me was a broader term than for most because *nothing* about my life seemed typical.

5
BODY AND BRAIN ERROR

When I came back to the barn and riding after having a stroke, I toned my horseback pursuits back to just show jumping. You know, because that is so much safer than eventing, right? After all, if you hit them, the big fences can fall down in show jumping, which is not necessarily the case on a solid cross-country course.

But the odds were against me. Even my passion—riding horses—wasn't connecting with me anymore. Despite having spent months in therapy to build back my body's strength and feeling, there was a disconnect between what I *could* do and what I *wanted* to do. It was like there was a "404 error" between my body and brain. *Page not found.*

I kept riding and practicing in the hopes I would improve. It was frustrating. In the winter of seventh grade, I entered my first competition post-stroke with a stocky, sluggish Haflinger/Quarter Horse cross named Spirit. While I was away, receiving treatments in California, my pony, Lacey, had been ridden by a trainer to keep her fit. The trainer noticed that Lacey was tripping a lot and had her examined by a veterinarian, who recommended retirement. Lacey enjoyed her new life, turned out with long-horned steers and donkeys, but it meant she was no longer able to train and compete with me, so I needed a new mount. Enter: Spirit. Competing had always been a goal with my riding. I knew I wanted to get back into the show ring.

It was time for a comeback, or so I thought. In the dead of winter, in the middle of Nowhere, Ohio, where the competition was being held only a few hours from my home in Michigan, it was freezing cold. The ground was littered with snow, and the arena footing had a slight crunch to it. The show was a *combined test*: the first day would be a dressage test and the second day would be jumping.

During our warmup the day before competition began, the show organizers decided it was the best time to test the arena microphone and speakers. Suddenly, the quiet of the ring was interrupted by a loud booming sound that resonated throughout the show grounds. The loud noise out of nowhere, or the echo that followed, resulted in my pony going vertical and then bucking me off, directly into the arena wall. It happened in the blink of an eye. One moment we were warming up, the next I was on the ground. I felt like one of those slime toys that you throw against the wall and watch slowly slide down as it buckles in on itself in a freeze-frame motion.

The dramatic fall didn't stop me, though. I somehow found the ability to stand up and get right back on to finish my warmup ride.

On dressage day, we felt great. Neither my pony nor I were worse for wear from the excitement the day before, and I, of course, was determined to keep going. To be honest, Spirit even felt a little lazy to me during our test. But ponies can be unpredictable.

The show jumping day was held in the facility's small indoor arena, perhaps thirty by seventy feet. It was cramped but necessary because of the inclement weather. It was filled to the brim with jumps and standards. Because of the tight fit, the course became more technical, and strides and balance mattered more than ever. Still, I wasn't concerned—I love a challenge. About halfway through the course, after a combination on the diagonal, my left leg caught Spirit by surprise on his barrel. The stroke had affected the left side of my body, and I didn't have as much feeling in it, so sometimes, it would do its own thing without my realizing. Spirit, according to his training, paid attention to what my leg had asked—its slight pressure told him to leg yield at the canter to the right. I never would have thought anything of it, and in a larger arena, the shift in our line might not have made a big difference, except for in our timing of our next jump.

To my right, a metal pasture gate formed an added barrier in front of the sliding arena doors. Because I was now blind in my right eye, I didn't see the doors or the gate until it caught me in its unyielding grip. Literally. Spirit had moved off my left leg, putting me directly against the metal gate. My right foot became stuck between the gate and the closed arena doors—lodged in between, unmoving. Feeling the resistance, Spirit bucked, and in a split second, everything went completely and utterly wrong.

I landed on the ground, screaming for my trainer. Not my mother, who was accustomed to my involuntary dismounts off my horse, but my trainer. In my mind, I had broken my leg, and all I could think was, *Oh my God, I'm a fucking pretzel. I'm a pretzel!*

Yelling this out loud, a twelve-year-old screaming profanity while on the ground in an unnatural position, probably shocked most attendees. Still, I think we should forgive cuss words in this instance.

My mother didn't even realize that I'd fallen off until she heard me scream, busy as she was trying to keep my two little brothers in line. I think the language I used to describe my state of being surprised even her, although she barely blinked at my colorful words. Calm as a cucumber, she said, "Sydney, it's just dislocated." She doesn't run from scary things because she doesn't want me to panic because *she's* freaked out.

Still, I don't know how she kept it together while I lay there with my right leg twisted the opposite direction from normal and up around my head. My right foot was on the left side of my head! I wasn't wrong. My body *was* a pretzel.

My trainer and mom covered me with coats to help prevent shock as I remained on the hard, freezing ground, waiting for medical help. It was a dinky little show with no ambulance on site, so someone had to call the emergency room at the closest hospital. It took about twenty minutes for the local paramedics to finally reach me, but I was in such a pickle that they said *they* couldn't touch me until the EMTs arrived, which made us wait even longer.

When one of the EMTs approached me, I looked up, and remembering what my mom had assured me, asked, "It's just dislocated, right?"

The guy looked at me in surprise and said, "Oh, no, honey! This is the worst femur break I've seen in my entire career. We must get this straightened out now or you could lose your leg."

The show was not only my first after my stroke, it was also right after my birthday (in November), and my gifts had been new winter breeches and riding boots, both of which were now splayed on the ground with me. The EMT asked me if he could cut my pants and boots, and I responded harshly, "No! This is my brand-new gear!" I don't know how I could still speak or function at that point, with the level of trauma my body was processing, but I knew I didn't want him ruining my new riding clothes. (I would be upset by such a suggestion to this day!)

The kind EMT tried to take my pants and boots off, but the pain was so excruciating, I finally gave in and gave permission for him to just cut them away. Losing my new gear devastated me, but the disappointment helped, in a way, because it gave me something to focus on besides the agony in my leg.

I had wanted to come back to horses and riding and just have things like they used to be—*before* my stroke. It was *this* that I'd been working so hard to do, and why I had been able to focus so hard on my physical therapy. The destruction of my new riding britches and boots didn't send me over the edge—it was the whole situation, and the sudden barrage of "what-ifs" that accumulated in my head as I dealt with this horrible experience.

What if I'd had more control of my left leg?

What if I could have seen out of my right eye and so avoided running into the metal gate?

What if, what if, what if?

But the events weren't something I could have controlled. Things happen...and sometimes, if you let go of thinking you could have somehow controlled them, they can strengthen you.

The truth was, my body was different from what it used to be, and I just had to accept it.

The stroke had forever changed my brain, and my heart just didn't want it to be true. I was no longer in sync with myself or my horse, something that was incredibly hard to acknowledge. Horses were the most important thing in life to me, and I'd already had so many setbacks to this point: first the diagnosis, then the unsuccessful treatments, then the stroke. Now, my "good" leg was twisted and unusable for months.

To me, at that moment, life seemed to be stacked against me.

It was a dark time in my life. The only constant source of happiness, besides my family, had been my riding, and now there seemed to be so many obstacles leaping in front of me, trying to derail me from my passion.

While I was recovering from the accident, sleeping in the living room downstairs in my family home and groggy with painkillers, I distinctly remember watching the Winter Olympics. (There wasn't a lot for me to do except watch television and drink Moose Tracks milkshakes.) I remember thinking, *These Olympians are out there striving for their own goals.* I hadn't found para dressage yet, and it didn't connect at that moment that I could be like those Olympians and Paralympians one day. However, I felt a kinship with them because I'd always had such a competitive drive, something that those amazing athletes needed to reach that pinnacle. I cheered them on from my lonely bed and imagined what it would be like to be a true athlete.

There was extensive damage to my femur from my collision with the gate, requiring surgery. To make matters worse, the pins necessary in the repair of the break were placed too low, forcing my leg to heal in a straight-out position. My "good" leg—the leg I *could* communicate with horses with—now couldn't be bent.

It was yet another blow to my fragile state of mind. I needed to go to extensive physical therapy to break through the scar tissue and start from scratch. Therapy was a constant for about eight months, but I kept pushing forward, undeterred, despite my incredibly low spirits. To keep me motivated, we tried something different: Spirit, the pony I'd fallen from at the show, became part of my rehabilitation for my injury. He had a wide barrel of a belly, which helped me by giving me a shape to bend my legs around. Riding him helped loosen the scar tissue, progressing mobility in the healing leg.

Spirit was my first "test" with adaptive riding, and while he was patient through my rehabilitation, my family and I realized he wasn't the right fit for it as a full-time job, as he didn't really want to do anything outside his "normal." We accepted he would not be the mount for me in the long run, and we needed to look further afield.

It broke my heart, as yet another thing from my childhood had to be left behind as I grew up too soon. Each of my early horses—Macy, Lacey, and Spirit—had helped mold me into the person I was gradually becoming.

Leaving them behind felt like saying goodbye to part of myself.

THERAPEUTIC RIDING AS A LIFELINE

Typical tweens and teenagers worry about grades, crushes, and fights with friends. I yearned to experience those things, but my life continued to be much more complicated than that.

I broke my ankle walking up the stairs just a few months after recovering from my riding accident, and I again needed a cast and yet *more* rehabilitation. (The ankle cast didn't keep me out of the saddle, though—shh, don't tell my doctor!)

Immediately following my stroke, occupational and physical therapy were a key part of me regaining my ability to walk and to use my left side again. With my dad for company, I had inpatient rehabilitation for that entire summer before returning home to Michigan. Once back, I began outpatient physical and occupational therapy. I dreaded doing occupational or physical therapy. It seemed like that was all I did. I had good days and bad days. The bad days far outnumbered the good days, so much so that I grew sour and difficult to deal with. My personality was much less "happy, social Syd" and much more of a dark, depressed teenager.

Hey, does that mean I was "typical"?

The only thing that kept me going back were my great relationships with my physical and occupational therapists. I especially loved occupational therapy because at the office, there was a kitchen. Baking and eating the gooey goodness that was the result of my labor was an added incentive. Therapies that didn't feel like "work" were most effective with me at this time. Repetitive exercises were boring, and it was harder for me to commit to those. But working on real-life tasks that could cause cookies to appear? *Yes, please.* I was willing to try.

I loved eating the desserts that we would bake in occupational therapy to such a degree that it forced me, no matter how much I hated it, to use my left arm, and the "treat reward" always gave me something to look forward to. I loved walking through the office after baking something yummy, handing it out to the other people and spreading just a little joy. Besides riding, baking was definitely my favorite thing to do in life.

My physical therapist, on the other hand, was a taskmaster. She always pushed me harder and asked me to use my left leg more than I even thought was possible. As a result, I regained a lot of mobility that I am sure I would not have if I didn't have access to such a great practitioner. It was her job to impel me to do more, and yes, sometimes anger could be a great catalyst for motivation! Personally, I preferred bribery with something sweet...but both methods got the job done, and I continued to improve.

Regaining my mobility and recovering after my stroke and accident were a challenge, and one that was exhausting, both physically and emotionally, for my whole family. Yet there were other challenges as well. Medical insurance was a big one; it was something we were always struggling with. When I had improved with my outpatient physical and occupational therapies and hit a plateau where I wasn't progressing as much, the insurance company decided that I had reached my "baseline," and that it was time for me to move to a home-based program.

The insurance company was only willing to pay for so much, and as a client, I was now limited in my choices for my ongoing health concerns.

My first wheelchair was a great example. It had become clear that I struggled to walk long distances, so it was decided it was necessary to work with my insurance to get a custom wheelchair—something that would work for me and my unique needs in the long term.

The Americans with Disabilities Act (ADA) prohibits discrimination against people with disabilities in everyday activities. Quickly, however, it became very clear that ADA laws and insurance guidelines are very antiquated and not set up for people with disabilities who want to live an active lifestyle.

When we applied for help purchasing a wheelchair, my insurance company replied that I could walk a half a mile, so there was no reason I would need one. After pressure from my parents, the company approved the *frame* of the wheelchair, but it was required that my mom appeal every single nut and bolt to build the wheelchair so that it would be functional for me. The episode was a stark reminder that advocating for equipment and care when you have unique needs can be a full-time job. Thousands of people face this dilemma daily, just to get what they need so that they can live a life that is accessible to them.

My foray into therapeutic riding was an accident. Life has a way of bringing things to you when the timing is right, even if the reason isn't clear in the moment of synchronicity.

I was struggling personally with accepting myself and my body, and the world accepting me in return. My mom saw how difficult reintegrating into my "new" life was. My body had been irrevocably changed, both through my trauma and the fact that I was no longer the small child I once had been. After my fall from Spirit, and then the rehab I did on him with some success, Mom suggested I take lessons at a therapeutic riding facility to help me find my balance again with horses—maybe, if found there, it would reflect on my life outside the barn. To me, horses had always been a "port in the storm," where I could focus my attention and forget about all the other things I couldn't control. Horses were a safety net I clung to for peace of mind. Life, for me, was going to be harsh—but perhaps I could find some stability in this one aspect that had always brought me joy.

Still, I was hesitant. I'd been *eventing*, which included galloping cross-country and jumping solid fences in open fields. Then, when it became necessary to scale back, I focused solely on show jumping, which even though it took place in a fenced arena still involved leaping over obstacles. To me, "therapeutic riding" seemed a little boring. I was a little "too cool for school" and initially fought the idea of it. In the end, though, I decided to at least try, because I had nothing else to lose.

Luckily, we found that Therapeutic Riding, Inc., in my home state of Michigan, embraced my previous experience with horses and supported me completely.

I started in a "traditional" way on what might be thought of as "typical" therapy lesson horses that were chosen for their stoic personalities and forgiving hearts. Therapy horses are truly angels on this earth for the work they do and the confidence they create in so many people with physical and mental disabilities or traumas.

As I spent time at the barn, speaking with the trainers and engaging in conversations about horses, they quickly sensed my experience level. It helped that I'm not exactly the "quiet type" and openly shared plenty of thoughts and stories! Also, the fact that I was able-bodied until I was 11 meant I had a completely different perspective and was never afraid to raise my voice and ask for what I needed.

When I'd found my seat on a horse again and felt ready to push myself, I asked my trainers at Therapeutic Riding, Inc., for a challenge.

The basic coordination exercises and hippotherapy were too easy for me. The trainers were very receptive to adapting my program in a way that would improve my riding skills to meet my needs. I was in a unique position because I had come to the barn with four years of eventing experience under my belt.

I think society encourages individuals with disabilities to be quiet. Many don't want to ask for help, cause problems, or worse, be "an inconvenience." Moreover, therapeutic riding programs are often hyperaware of "staying within the protocol" and keeping activities extremely safe—not that there is anything wrong with that. But I believe there is so much more potential for riders to learn and compete using adaptive measures "outside the box," and not just focused on a prescribed program.

The cultural difference between the protective bubble placed around those with disabilities who ride horses in the United States and other countries was starkly apparent a few years later when I went to try a horse in Germany.

When it became clear that Spirit was not comfortable with my body post-stroke the way we needed him to be, we realized it was time to look for a horse for the "new" me. Outside of my time at Therapeutic Riding, Inc., I continued riding with my original trainer, a no-nonsense German with no experience with therapeutic riding or para dressage. We planned a trip to Germany to try to find the "perfect horse." (The United States commonly imports horses from Germany for use in equestrian sports. A 2020 article in the journal *Society and Animals* reported that "over $300 million dollars in horses are imported into the United States, and over a third comes from Germany.") None of us considered how my trainer would know what my body needed without any experience with adaptive riding—we just rolled with it. It was thrilling. I had never been out of the country other than driving through part of Canada on my way to my grandparents' house in Maine. It was the opportunity of a lifetime.

Before you think I and my family were being dramatic, going "all the way to Germany to find a horse," it's important to note we had attempted to try a few horses in the United States, but my trainer and I had met with a lot of resistance when I showed up with braces on my left arm and left leg. Immediately, sellers would refuse to go forward with the trial, informing us their liability insurance didn't cover someone with a disability, and I couldn't ride their horses. This was incredibly disheartening. I already felt different in a body that wasn't yet "my own," and now I was being judged, the assumption being that based on my appearance, I could not ride safely. To me, it seemed everyone was just afraid of getting sued. I may not have been "able-bodied," but I was a skilled rider.

In Europe, horse sale barns were more open to me riding than those in my own country. Instead of resistance, those in Germany met us with excitement, eager for me to get on and try their horses. I didn't need to sign a waiver to protect them or me. When I asked, "So…I can just get on the horse?" they looked at me blankly, seemingly surprised by the question, and retorted, "You fall off a horse just like anyone else, yes?"

It was a breath of fresh air to be treated the same as other riders, regardless of my physical limitations. Individuals with disabilities aren't porcelain dolls who have to play it safe all the time. If someone, and especially a child, wants to push themselves to be better, then we should foster that person's talent and desire.

In Germany, I saw many sights, ate so much good food, and rode so many talented horses. Trying horses is always a challenge for me, not because of my physical disabilities, but because I fall in love with almost every horse that I ride. In Germany, however, there were two that really stuck out. One was interesting because, while he wasn't anything show-stopping, he had such an understanding mind. And then, on the very last day of our trip, I had a chance to ride the most gorgeous mare. All my expectations were just blown away. She had that adaptable mind I needed while being fancy. She was everything I had been looking for, and was undoubtedly *the one*. On the flight back to Michigan, I couldn't stop thinking about her.

Alas, it all fell apart, as things so often do with horse deals—especially

  BEYOND EXPECTATIONS

international horse deals. The mare had *piroplasmosis*, a tick-born blood disease, which, when treated, can be managed in most cases. But it meant she could not be imported to the United States.

My search for the right equine partner continued.

Therapeutic Riding, Inc., had a cousin of a famous eventing horse named Theodore O'Connor in the barn. ("Teddy" had become famous because as a legit pony—just over 14 hands—he competed at the highest levels of international eventing with his rider, Olympian Karen O'Connor.) No other student could ride "Robbie," a liver chestnut gelding, because he was hot and forward. Eventually, however, my trainer allowed me to work with him.

It was a defining moment.

The first time I got to ride Robbie, I was giddy like a fangirl. He was being warmed up at the canter as I walked into the indoor riding arena, and my jaw dropped when I heard I was getting the opportunity to ride him. As a child who had grown up eventing, Teddy O'Connor was a kind of hero of mine. He did so many amazing things in a small body! I could relate to that! My family and I had traveled to the big international three-day event in Lexington to watch him. Being allowed to ride a horse related to Teddy gave me a sense of pride and accomplishment that I hadn't felt in a long time.

Putting my foot in the stirrup, I couldn't stop the smile on my face, and I didn't try. Robbie was so smooth, but very forward, and I could feel him coiled and ready to go underneath me. The first time I jumped him, I once again felt that feeling I knew so well from my eventing days—like I was flying. For a moment, I forgot that my body was fighting against me. It felt like freedom.

That the facility and my trainer trusted me and my horse experience, even with my limitations, was a huge vote of confidence. I felt empowered for the first time in a long while, and it was a huge step forward in regaining my belief in myself. Because they embraced me, it was easier for me to embrace the idea of therapeutic riding, and the changes in my body, in return.

Instead of teaching me to ride with a disability or having me do physical therapy on horseback, Therapeutic Riding, Inc., did something much more. They were an integral part of helping me adapt to the body that I now had. Yes, they gave me tools to become better at riding, but besides my family, they were the first to treat me like I was special, not because of my condition or my stroke, but because I was capable of so much. They allowed me to blossom and gave me the tools to do so.

To trust me with a horse like Robbie, when they didn't trust others, was a gift that changed the trajectory of my life. I felt "good enough" for the first time in a very long while.

The National Center for Equine Facilitated Therapy (NCEFT) defines *adaptive riding* as "recreational horseback riding and horsemanship lessons adapted for each individual's unique needs/goals and ability." Many therapeutic riding centers will have basic "adaptive equipment," such as "rainbow reins," with color markers so riders can visualize where their hands need to be, or surcingles with a handles for side-walkers to hold and stabilize the balance of rider. But there are so many other options available to those with unique needs. It was eye-opening for me that with a few equipment adjustments, I could ride just as well as I used to.

I had a Benik neoprene brace on my left arm to keep my thumb open and my wrist straight. My trainers helped me adapt my brace with a flap to increase my grip so I could hold the reins. I learned to use "looped" or "ladder" reins so I could hold the reins with one hand but still use direct rein contact to communicate with my horse's mouth, as opposed to neck reining with side-to-side pressure on his neck. These modifications opened the door to a bigger world available to me. My body was different, but I could still *ride*, and *ride well*, which allowed me to open my wings once again and fly. I'd always thrived and pushed myself competitively. I could now continue to dream. I just had to be open to changes in how the dream might take shape.

Years later, Therapeutic Riding, Inc., would become a United States Equestrian Federation (USEF) Para-Equestrian Dressage Center of Excellence (COE). Centers of Excellence are riding centers designed to grow the sport of para dressage throughout the United States. They hold clinics for riders to become familiar with the sport and to bridge the gap between therapeutic riding and para dressage. They are helping identify riders out there who, with the right resources and knowledge, could be the future of the sport.

Therapeutic Riding, Inc., became a bridge from my old life to my new one. At the barn, I was *capable*, and my confidence in the saddle grew.

But middle school was increasingly difficult. There were ramps for my wheelchair at school, but they were so steep, I couldn't get up them without help. Yet, my friends were forbidden to help me because their assistance was considered a liability. My friends grew tired of waiting for me and left me behind. I felt so adrift and lonely.

My occupational therapist saw my internal struggle and recommended a support group. It was not specifically for young people; in fact, I was the only one under twenty years old in the group. My mother encouraged me to go because she felt it might help me realize there were others "like me" in the world. All teenagers can be narcissistic, and in my case, with my health issues and general life upheaval, it would have been easy to feel alienated by society and retreat behind a protective shell.

Instead, with the encouragement of my family, the affirmations of therapeutic riding, and now, a support group filled with others with similar challenges, I felt like I could finally move forward and explore my world. It was in a different way than I'd done it before, but that didn't have to mean that it was less powerful. Joining the support group was a way of me reaching out rather than retreating, and it enabled me to see that others were carrying out their own goals, despite the challenges life might have thrown at them. It was possible to live a normal, successful life. It just looked a little different from the usual picture.

The support group gave me perspective and a place to share my experiences where I felt comfortable. Being around other people like me not only inspired me, it motivated me to try and inspire others. It gave me hope for a future, perhaps different from what I had once imagined, but one that I was beginning to feel like I could make just as beautiful.

THE DARK MIDDLE SCHOOL VIBE

Late in the summer before my seventh-grade year started, my brother Simon's best friend from preschool, Jason, came from South Korea with his sister, Jennifer, and his mom, Jinhee, for a long visit (they had moved back several years before). We were so happy to welcome them into our home, and it was a nice bit of community after a very stressful time. I was twelve, Alex was ten, Simon and Jason were eight, and Jennifer was six years old. I *loved* it. Not only was I the oldest (and obviously the wisest), but I finally got to play at having a little sister. I was also assigned to be the babysitter and the "adult" at home while my mom and Jinhee ran errands in the afternoons. For just a short time each day, my parents gave me autonomy and responsibility. Knowing that my mom, dad, and Jinhee trusted me enough to look after everyone further boosted my confidence.

Those summer days became a blur of so much fun and a lot of chaos—in the best of ways. They had a pleasant rhythm. I got up early for breakfast and so we could rush to the barn for chores and riding time before the heat of the day. While Mom and I were there, Simon, Alex, Jason, and Jennifer would wake up leisurely, eat breakfast, and then...*study*! Doing homework over summer! It horrified my brothers, but Jinhee was a taskmaster with school. I later learned that their South Korean school system made it necessary for her to be so. Jason and Jennifer had no room for a summer break, or they'd fall behind.

When Mom and I returned home from the barn, we kids would often take a break from the heat and swim in the pool the moms set up for us. If not the pool, we'd bounce on the trampoline. Our yard was the best in the entire neighborhood! All the kids would come over and swim, jump on the trampoline, or just hang out. It was the most amazing summer, and something I needed to heal.

Jinhee was the best cook. She was always making *kimbap* (seaweed rice rolls), and other delicious South Korean dishes, like no one's business. I still remember the giant box of South Korean food she brought with her, both to give to and make for us; then, right before they returned to South Korea, she did a large grocery run and filled three suitcases with Costco goodies!

One moment from their visit is hard to forget—I can look back on it and laugh now, but at the time, it was so embarrassing!

It was a hot and dusty day at the barn, so my mom and I rushed into the house after my lesson to take showers and feel a little more human. My shower was not yet adjusted for the changes in my body post-stroke, and it included a step into a tub, which was always quite slippery, so it came with its own risks. Midway through my shower, all soaped up, I lost my footing and found myself flopped *out* of the shower, wedged uncomfortably between the tub and the toilet.

Not ideal.

These are the glamorous moments that come with a newfound disability. I was soapy, naked, and very stuck. I yelled for help since I had wedged my good arm into the wall, and I couldn't work it loose from my angle without someone's help. Much to my shock, it wasn't my mom who came to save my soapy teenage butt, but Jinhee! She swooped in, picked me up, and gently placed me back in the shower, all within the blink of an eye and before either of us could even say anything.

We had many good laughs over the situation after the fact, and I'll always be grateful for no-nonsense help in what could have been a really uncomfortable moment for me.

Middle school was rocky, to say the least. No one at that age has it easy. Leaving elementary school means more work academically, but more than that, it's the Wild West for social anxiety. Hormones take the wheel, and everyone, with very few exceptions, has an awkward stage. I started out totally able-bodied in sixth grade—despite my Wyburn-Mason diagnosis—with no actual idea that could or would ever change. The summer before seventh grade, my stroke altered me mentally and physically. Suddenly, I was wearing a leg brace and using a wheelchair. I was completely different from the person who had left school for summer break the spring before.

It was nerve-racking, rolling up to school on the first day. I had refused to be administered a steroid to treat my migraine due to the trauma the side effects had caused when I was younger. However, the pain I regularly experienced from my incessant migraine and brain inflammation became so intense the doctors pushed the issue until I finally relented. The steroid gave me severe acne that was swollen and painful, flaking off my skin. It humiliated me. I had to get a note from my doctor to be allowed to wear a hat in school that would partially cover my face. All I yearned to do was blend into the sea of tall, seemingly perfectly able-bodied middle schoolers. "Standing out" is never good at that age, and it can easily make you a target for ridicule or bullying. I was not usually a self-conscious person at all, but my body was already so different from the others—I was wearing a leg brace and using a wheelchair—weight gain and acne was the icing on the cake.

I was unrecognizable to my peers.

My middle school had two accessibility ramps. The daredevil I am, it stoked me at the time that I'd be able to zoom down them in my wheelchair. Unfortunately, I found out quickly that the school administration was not nearly as excited as I was for this possibility. There were disputes between the school and my parents during this time—a lot of messages and meetings.

I was labeled a liability, something we had now heard several times, and I wasn't self-sufficient, because I needed help to push my wheelchair up ramps. In a nutshell, I was no longer welcome to attend the school. Discrimination was new to me, and it was a real shock. Academically, I was the same student, but my physical needs were very real, and the school wasn't willing or able to make allowances for those changes. It tempted me to run over some toes accidentally...on purpose.

Sadly, I lost most of my school friends who didn't know how to accept the changes in me. My closest friend for years just faded away. I remember the day I sent her five texts. I didn't realize that she would never reply again. Finally, my mother sat me down and asked me to stop trying to hold on to someone who clearly didn't want to know me anymore. "She's not worth your time," Mom said. But I was heartbroken. We had spent every day together the year before. Then she just disappeared, and our friendship was over, like it had never happened at all.

I had changed drastically while my schoolmates experienced typical adolescence and could not relate to me. My new body, my old friends, and the school's rigid authority figures alienated me from the school. Social anxiety and daily difficulties affected more than just my confidence; they affected my grades, as well. I found school to be more challenging, especially in math. My dad would spend hours tutoring me, patiently trying to help me focus and improve academically.

It was a very dark time in my life.

However, it wasn't all terrible. They say in adversity you find out who your true friends are. It is so true. I found a few students who learned to celebrate my differences rather than be uncomfortable with them. I'm friends with many of them still to this day. When life gets hard, it's the friends that stand by you that matter.

◇ ◇ ◇

I was in regular classes with an Individualized Education Plan or Program (IEP) for my vision issues, but overall remained tracked with most students. One of the coolest benefits of being blind in my right eye was that we incorporated braille—the tactile writing system—into my IEP. Let me tell you, it is so hard! Most people read braille with two hands, and doing so with one hand, like I had to, was especially tricky, but it was also a fun challenge.

Gym class, however, was the bane of my existence. I had to attend the class for credit but was told to just sit on the sidelines, which only made me feel more excluded. As an adult I love adaptive fitness, but at my middle school there were no attempts to include me in even the smallest ways. I was just the "disabled girl" who was only allowed to watch.

My science teacher, on the other hand, tried to include me in his class. Even better, he seemed to really get my sense of humor. When I told other students not to bring equipment near me because I was "radioactive" (my attempt at a self-deprecating joke about my outsider status), he'd just laugh and go along with it. I had so much fun with it. During a unit when we were studying electricity, I offered to bring in the unit that used electrical stimulation (e-stim) in my physical therapy. My teacher agreed. All the tough jocks asked to put the e-stim on their faces and crank it up, but they couldn't handle it— and I laughed at them. They probably thought it was easy for me, so as a result, it would be easy for them. Little did they know how strong I really was.

I love to laugh, so I entertained myself by telling a lot of tall tales to my fellow students, trying to get a reaction out of them. Humor was a deflection, but more, it's just not in my nature to hold grudges or be negative. Attention on my terms became the goal. I began to embrace more alternative fashion styles. All black everything! If I was going to be made to feel like an outsider, I would dress how I wanted, and black matched my mood.

◇ ◇ ◇

The students I could most easily relate to were those in what was considered "special education"—classes and instruction specially designed to meet the unique needs of individuals with disabilities. I wasn't technically "one of them" because the program at my school was geared toward learning behaviors and challenges, as opposed to physical limitations, but I gravitated to these kids who were also on the outside. More, the special education classroom became an oasis of sorts where I didn't feel judgment. We all had something that set us apart.

I made friends with a lot of the kids, helped daily in their classroom on my own time, and volunteered at their summer school program. I craved a group to fit into, and they made me feel accepted. I could also see how our school was teaching them that they, like me, were different from the "regular" kids, and it fueled anger inside me. I knew what it was like to have once been physically capable and considered part of the general school population, rather than the fringe. It was a huge wakeup call to suddenly be on the other side.

When I look back, I was once part of the majority that didn't embrace the "outsiders." I remember how, before my stroke, the "other" kids were off in their own room, set apart from me and the rest of the mainstream school population, and didn't interact with us. After my stroke, I had a new perspective. I could see both sides of the social equation because I had lived on both sides.

I became so passionate about the kids I got to know that I considered one day becoming a special education teacher myself. But I soon knew that I wanted to do more than focus my attention on small groups of students. I believe we need access and education reform on the national level, and I want to be an advocate on a larger scale. While we've made great strides in the last decade, there is a potential for so much more to help integrate young people with physical and mental challenges and adapt the world for them, rather than separate and exclude them.

Years later, when I was in high school, I ran into a girl named Annie with Down syndrome who I had spent time helping in middle school, and she remembered me. That I had made a happy, lasting memory for this young woman is something that I will treasure always. I had found peace in her world, set apart as it was, and that I gave her peace in return is a gift. Helping others to see they weren't so different, even if our learning institution made them feel that way, helped me focus less on my own troubles.

This was a defining moment in school and in my desire for advocacy in educational institutions and everyday life. All I wanted was a place to fit in, but in finding one, a door to a new purpose opened.

Those who are facing physical or mental challenges don't belong in the "broken" pile. We may have different needs than others, but we still have a lot to contribute!

FINDING THE FIRE

My mother searched the internet for something to help bring me back from the abyss after I broke my leg. I was going through a pure funk and my anger was toxic—what I *wanted* to do didn't align with what my body *could* do. It frustrated me greatly, and I think Mom realized how dangerous it could get for me. She knew that I needed something to help me embrace my body *as it was* post-stroke.

To put it plainly, I was struggling. Thank goodness for the internet!

In a low-key way, Mom mentioned in passing, "Para dressage is happening for the first time at the World Equestrian Games in Kentucky this year. I got tickets for Grammy, you, and me to go watch!"

While she hoped that this surprise trip would resonate and give me hope, something I didn't have a lot of at that time, my initial reaction was, "Dressage? That's so boring, they aren't even jumping over anything." After all, I had loved the thrill and adrenaline of eventing, but dressage had been my least favorite of the three phases. (It didn't help I was an ornery twelve-year-old.) Begrudgingly, I agreed to go.

We drove from Ann Arbor to Lexington, Kentucky, and stayed at a Holiday Inn near the Kentucky Horse Park to be close to the festivities.

I can still smell the incredible cinnamon rolls we would have each morning before heading to the Horse Park during that trip. When I smell cinnamon rolls now, it at once jolts me with core memories of what became a pivotal moment in my life. It's funny how certain things stay in your brain. At the time there was nothing better than gooey goodness for breakfast, followed by a day spent watching horses.

We'd been to the Kentucky Three-Day Event, held at the same location, every spring since I could remember, and we thought we knew the Park like the back of our hands. We were wrong. The crowd for the World Equestrian Games (WEG) was enormous, with far more disciplines represented, and therefore spectators, than for the Kentucky Three-Day. It made our former experience seem dinky in comparison.

We stumbled our way around without my wheelchair. I was using a cane, but I'd forgotten how vast the Park was and quickly got tired. My family had unintentionally pushed me into a situation where I had to walk a long distance, as we got lost repeatedly, and it annoyed me. Being as stubborn as I am, though, I refused to admit defeat and accept a ride on one of the golf carts passing by. (I think stubbornness is my superpower and has kept me from giving up a number of times throughout my life.)

Finally, after we were all tired and sweaty, we found the indoor arena where the para dressage competition was taking place. It felt gigantic—I have never been in another that struck me with its scale in that way since.

I had no idea when I walked through those doors that the rest of my life was about to greet me.

 BEYOND EXPECTATIONS

My first view as we walked into the shade of the indoor was of a rider from Great Britain, Ricky Balshaw, just hanging out by the rail, watching the other competitors. He was cute, with blond hair and tattoos! What can I say? I seized the opportunity. I walked right up to him and said, "How's it going?"

Suddenly this trip and the sport of para dressage looked a lot more appealing.

I can't do justice to the feeling I had when I saw the para riders for the first time. These were athletes with disabilities like me, competing at the upper levels. My earlier childhood goals didn't seem so far away anymore. For the first time in what felt like years, I felt my inner fire rekindle deep within. It may have been a small flame, but it wasn't gone like I'd feared.

The rider I remember the most, the one who really affected me, was a woman without arms. She held one set of the reins of the double bridle in her mouth, and the second set of reins with her bare feet, and she rode *beautifully*. I'd never seen a more striking example of inclusivity as that woman in my life. Nothing was stopping her from achieving her goals, and it made me feel like I could do the same thing.

I had a true epiphany, just like a moment out of a movie! I stood there watching and thought, *If these athletes are out there pursuing their goals, then I can do it too. If I really apply myself, it could be me on this team.*

It was the most empowering moment of my life to date. Even though I was different, I wasn't as useless as society seemed to be telling me I was.

I don't know if my mother was prepared for how excited I'd be after so many months of depression. She had booked our trip to help me through a very dark time, and like a switch, suddenly, my social self came back to the fore. It made all the difference to be around people who made me feel "normal" once again.

I wasn't different. I wasn't the odd one out.

For the first time in a long time, I had hope. My mother thought she'd opened Pandora's Box, but there was no turning back for me. I'm forever grateful to her for recognizing my need for a community who understood my experiences with individuals working toward goals like mine.

It wasn't enough to watch others ride at WEG. I wanted to meet as many riders as possible. I went from shuttered, surly, teenage Sydney, to excited, chatty Syd in the blink of an eye. My mom and grandma probably had whiplash. I had an absolute blast!

My mom and grandma stayed in the background and let me explore, giving me freedom. I enjoyed every moment and met as many people as possible. It's easy to coddle your disabled child and try to protect them from the world, perpetuating dependence. My family didn't helicopter me or wrap me in bubble wrap like I was some broken thing. Instead, they gave me free rein and let me explore. I've always been my own person. I am so grateful to them for allowing that independence to evolve.

That independence allowed me to walk up, limping the whole way and leaning on my cane, to anyone and everyone who was around, so that I could introduce myself and say hello. I knew the sport of para dressage was a way that I could step up to the challenges I was facing and not let life beat me down. It became apparent that it gave me the strength to embrace my new body and my new self. It was the beginning of something exciting.

One of these introductions became life-changing.

I opened with, "You look like someone I should know."

I am so damn cheeky, but it would be the most important meeting of my life. That rider turned out to be Jonathan Wentz, who would set a cascade of events into motion that led me to where I am today.

At the time, Jonathan was about nineteen years old and representing the United States at his first World Equestrian Games. He had the sunniest disposition—so friendly and welcoming. At over six feet tall you might think he would seem unapproachable, but he had a presence about him, an energy, a way of making others feel comfortable— something I emulate to this day and hope to provide for others.

Jonathan's goal to be a positive light and help bring more young riders into the sport of para dressage quickly became apparent. It was his passion, and it was something that really resonated with me. Before I knew it, he offered to introduce me to Hope Hand, founder and (then) president of the United States Para-Equestrian Association (USPEA), so that I could be "classified," right then, right there—at the World Equestrian Games! (According to the FEI, classification by "Grade" enables competitors to be judged at an international level on their individual skill on their horse, regardless of their physical impairment. "The competitor's mobility, strength, and coordination are assessed in order to establish their Classification Profile. People with similar functional ability Profiles are grouped into competition Grades. For para dressage, the Grades range from Grade I for the most severely impaired, to Grade V for the least impaired.")

My grandmother was with me during my chat with Jonathan, while my mother remained on the other side of the arena. As I felt my life suddenly being swept up in a current that might lead to a future I hadn't thought possible, I hurried back to where my mom was waiting.

"Mom, Mom!" I said, my voice full of excitement and disbelief. "You'll never believe this but I'm going to get classified right here for para dressage and start doing *this*! Right now!"

Before she could utter a word, I was off again.

After Jonathan's ride, he took me to meet Hope, as promised, and get classified. I did not know what to expect. I assumed the process would happen on a horse, where I was most comfortable—I imagined maybe I'd even get to ride Richter Scale, the horse Jonathan had just competed. I was so hyped.

To my disappointment, there was no horse. Watching other riders is never the same as being on a horse myself, so it bummed me out. Any day I can get on the back of a horse is a good day. Later, physical therapists trained as classifiers explained that being on a horse can make someone look more able-bodied than that person actually is, so classifiers base their evaluation on the rider only, unmounted.

The classifiers at WEG led me to a trailer, with my grandma in tow as chaperone. There I did a series of muscle tests to help determine what "Grade" I would be when competing in para dressage, so that I would ride with athletes who had similar abilities on an even playing field.

I remember thinking, *Is this actually happening?*

I was classified as a Grade II rider, so I would ride tests that included fifty-fifty walk and trot requirements, parallel to a Second Level dressage test, minus the canter aspect. I felt elation. I hadn't even known this sport existed a month ago! In the blink of an eye, my mindset changed from believing dressage was boring to appreciating all the potential there was for me in the sport.

"Mom, Grammy, next WEG and Paralympics—it's going to be me on that team," I announced.

If my change of attitude surprised my family after our trip to WEG, they didn't show it. In fact, they were likely just relieved I had a new, positive focus. Many kids have big dreams for their futures. I was no exception. And I've always been determined and goal-oriented. When I said I was going to work toward a goal, I put all my passion into accomplishing it.

My diagnosis and stroke would not define me anymore. I wanted to write the rest of my story.

1. At seven, Pony Club became a massive part of my life. It was where I learned about horses and formed close friendships. Macy and I even helped my team win at a show jumping rally with a record breaking twenty-six-second jump off!

2. When I first started riding, I thought flatwork was boring. Little did I know! Here I'm on Macy. What she lacked in size, she made up in heart.

3. My parents were my biggest support system at a time when I needed them the most.

4. With my dad and brothers, Simon and Alex, on one of our many trips to California for my treatment. (Note my *glasses*! Did I need them? No. Did I get them anyway? Heck yes!)

5 & 6. Family support and beautiful views helped us through those tough early treatment days, and my parents always knew how to cheer me up! We are with my grandparents (left) and on a beach riding adventure (below).

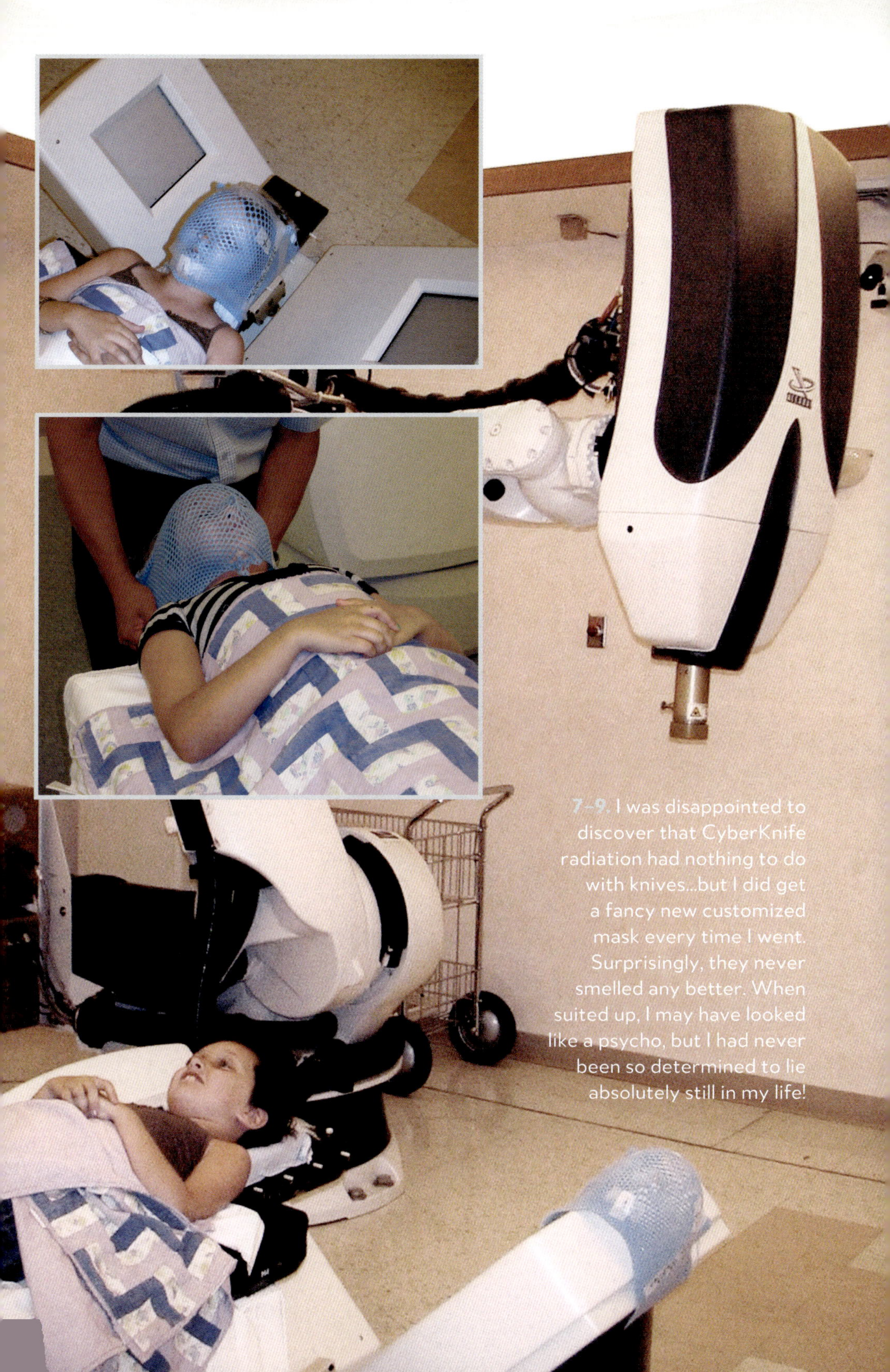

7-9. I was disappointed to discover that CyberKnife radiation had nothing to do with knives...but I did get a fancy new customized mask every time I went. Surprisingly, they never smelled any better. When suited up, I may have looked like a psycho, but I had never been so determined to lie absolutely still in my life!

10. When I say "cheese grater dock," I mean it! The ramp to the dock at my grandparents' house in Maine was treacherous.

11. With my brothers on "Otter Island," as we called it, in Maine. Obviously, we're related…

12 & 13.
When in Maine, my brothers and I had different ideas about accessorizing.

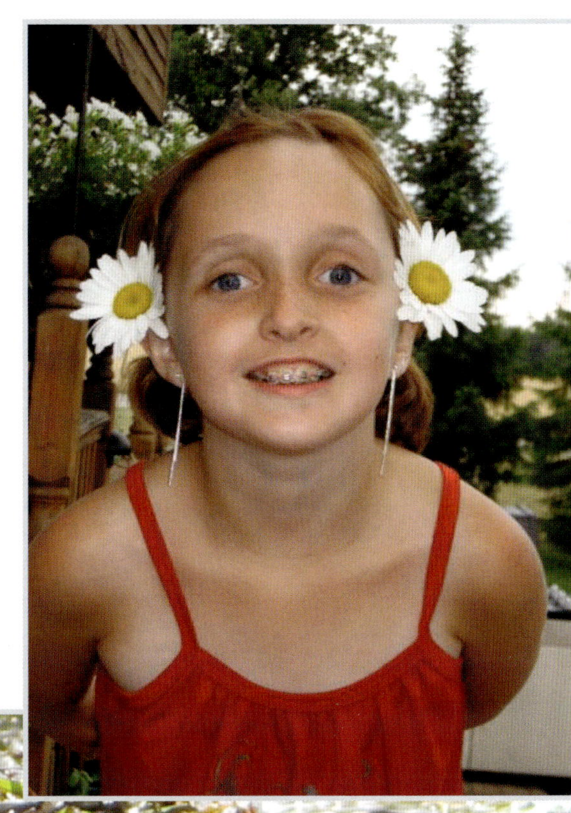

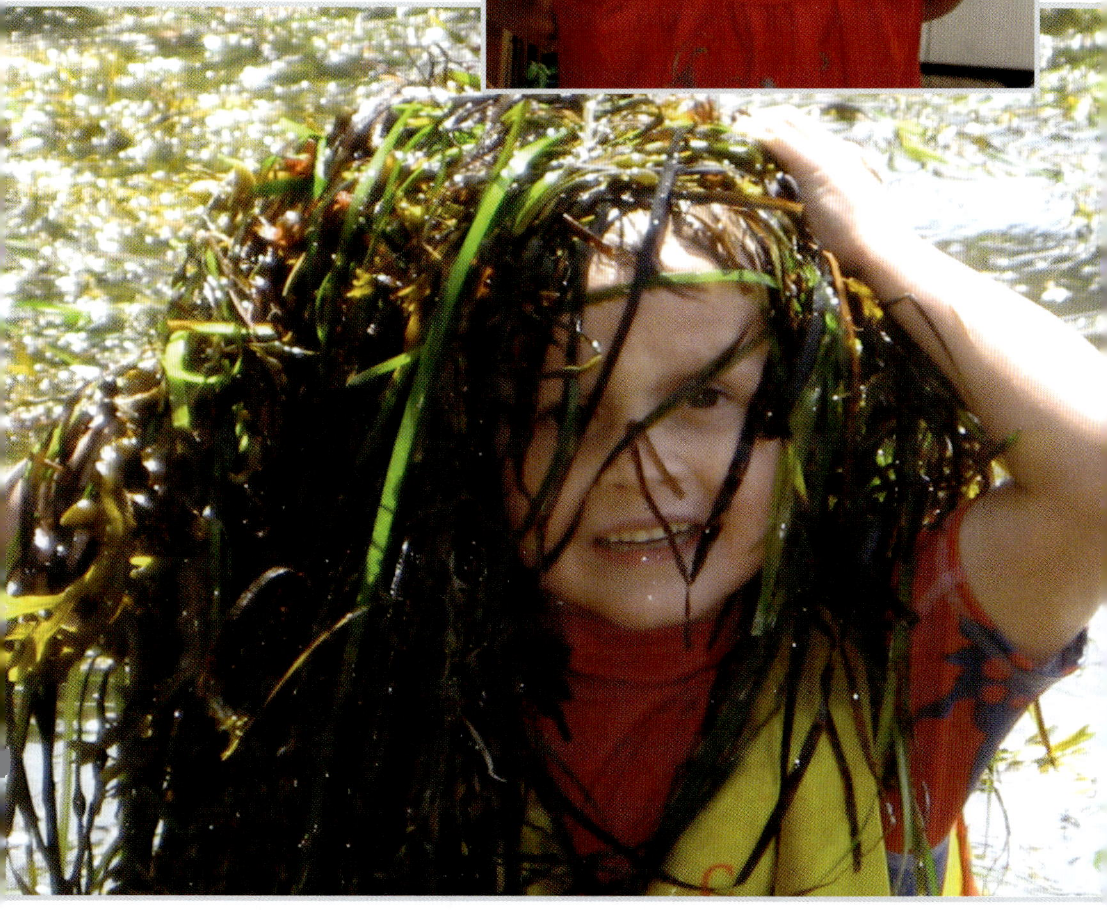

14. Riding horses cross-country didn't come without it's risks, including a bad fall that resulted in a serious concussion, but I loved every single moment out there on course!

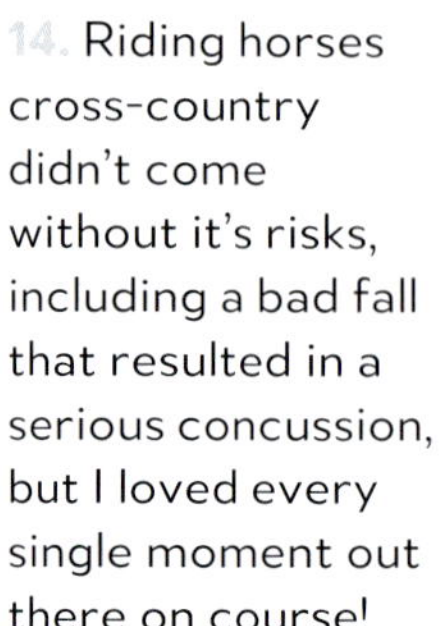

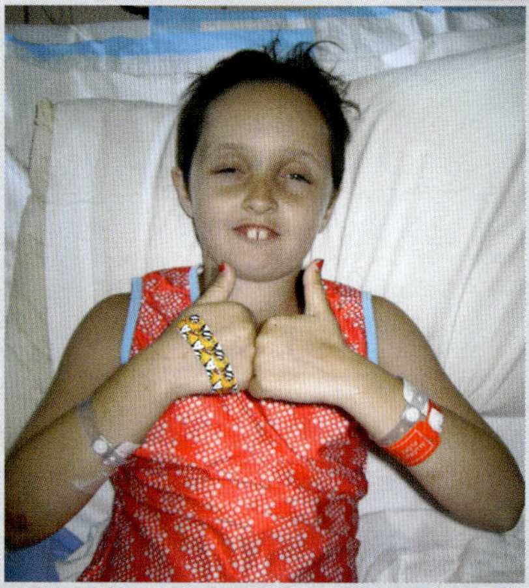

15 & 16. Lacey (above and below) was a mare full of heart and personality. A challenging day for me could immediately be turned into a fantastic day with one ride. We didn't get the opportunity to enter a lot of shows due to my medical treatments, but when we did it was pure magic!

17–19. The onset of my migraines when I was ten was one of the most challenging times of my life to date, and the only time that I have ever experienced a pain so intense that, some days, I physically couldn't get out of bed, let alone ride. Our search for any type of solution from my doctors ended up with me overly prescribed with little relief. But one thing I've never let my condition take away from me is a general positive attitude. I try to find a way to smile, no matter what I am experiencing!

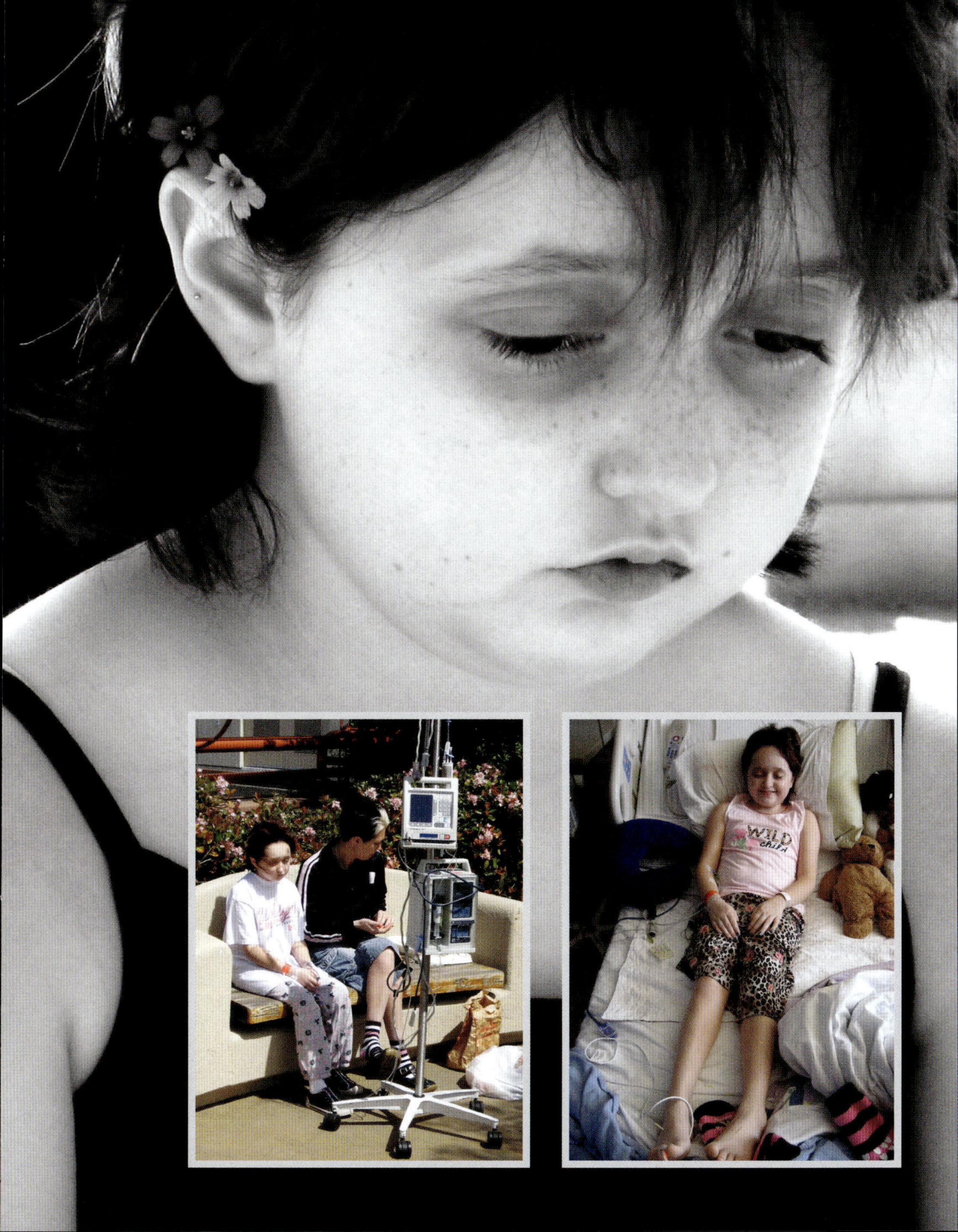

20–22. Prior to my first stroke, I got a taste of eventing competition with Spirit. Dressage was his favorite of the three phases. But he also decided he liked cross-country because of the lush grass all around. (I loved the speed!) Show jumping was fun for both of us, but where was the grass when he was in need of a snack?

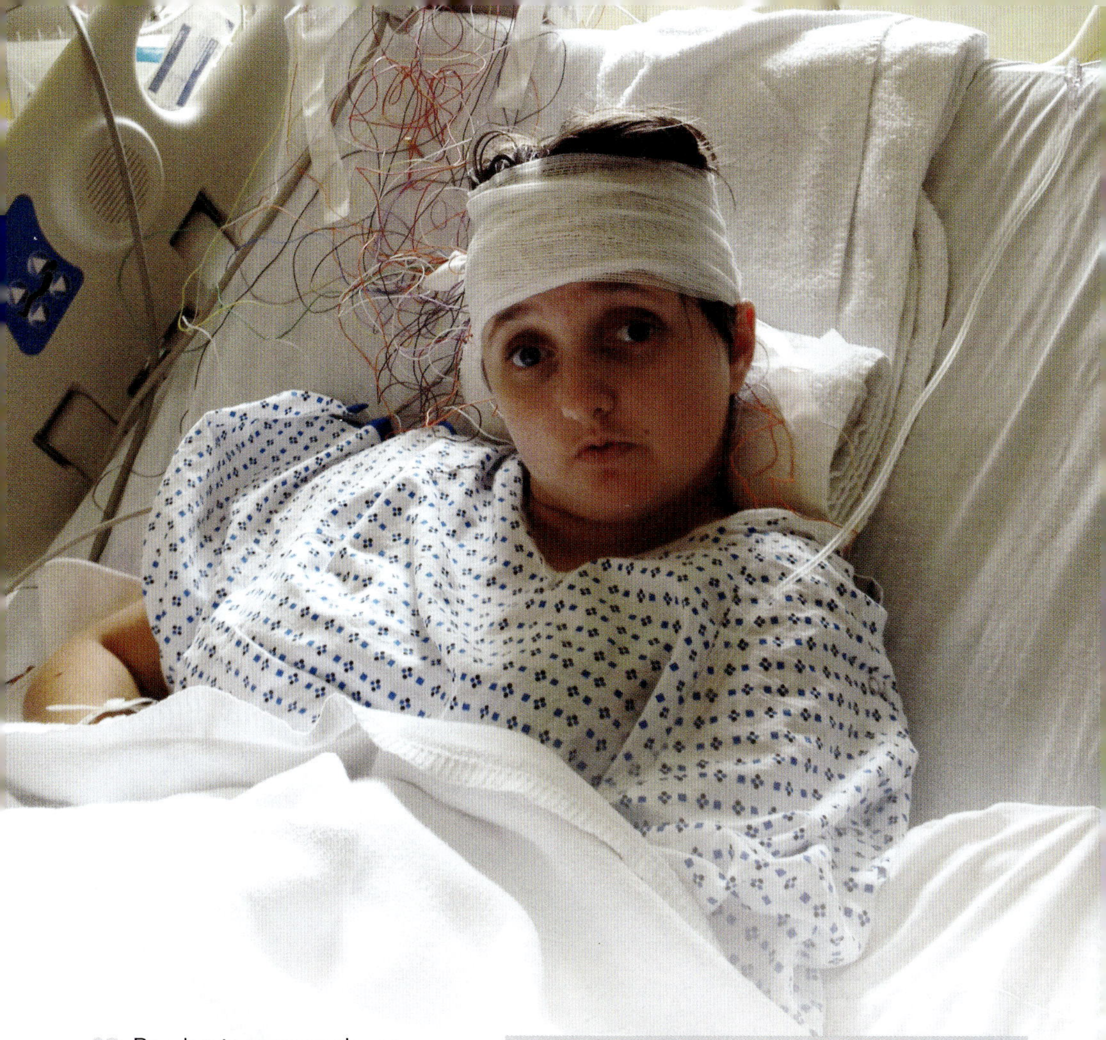

23. Pre-brain-surgery I was
hooked up to electronic
transmitters to give the doctors
a glimpse inside my head. Boy,
did they hurt coming off and
pulling my hair with them.

24. Christmas after I broke
my femur from a fall from
Spirit was spent in my bed in
the living room—not exactly
what kids dream of.

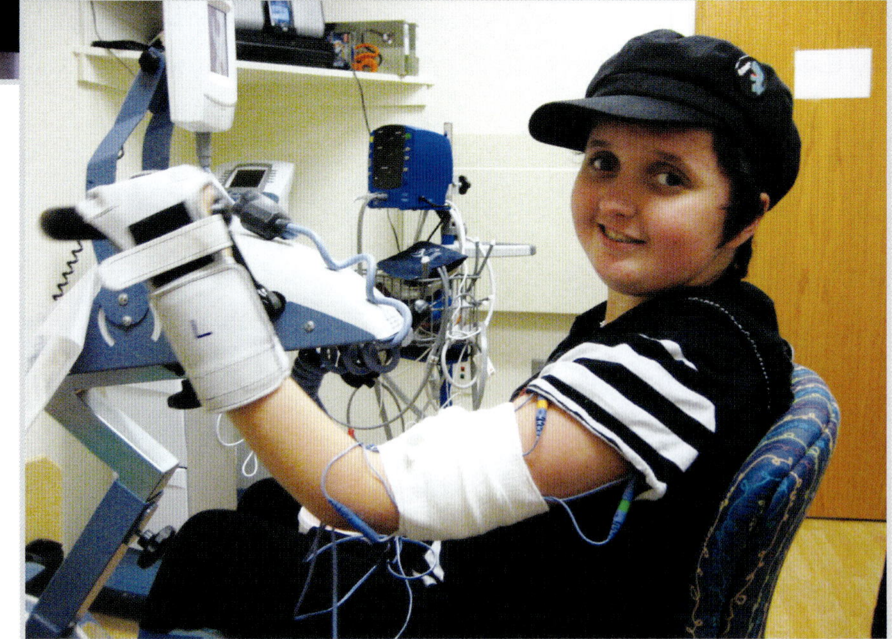

25. Although I didn't have a ton of friends during my middle school years, the friendships I did have were near and dear to my heart. Here I am with Maddie at eighth grade graduation.

26. After my first stroke, hours were spent in physical and occupational therapy, working to reconnect neural pathways that had been impacted or shut down.

27. Don't mind me, just a twelve-year-old "fangirling" over British Paralympian Ricky Balshaw! Still, slightly embarrassed by that…

28. Chip had my heart from the moment he gave me his very first hug.

29. Because my family couldn't afford to transport Chip around the country to shows, I had to "catch ride." Pegasus was a very understanding and calm stallion I competed several times. I felt honored to have the opportunity to catch ride a horse of his stature!

30. Chip and I entering the show ring together for the first time.

31. When Chip and I practiced for a demonstration ride at what was then the North American Junior Young Rider Championships, the Rolex Arena at the Kentucky Horse Park was the biggest arena I had ever ridden in. I was only twelve, and the size of the ring made me feel even younger!

32. I had gone from spectating at shows at the Kentucky Horse Park, to riding my own horse there at the Championships. It was surreal!

BRINGING HOME PARA DRESSAGE

That trip to Kentucky irrevocably changed me. It was a shift to a path that challenged me, that pushed me to work hard every day, and that allowed me the freedom to ride horses like I'd always dreamed. My father noticed the difference in me immediately when we returned home. He turned to my mother and said, "Well, you got her fire back, I guess!"

He was right. I had a new life goal and a new sparkle in my soul.

My then-trainer was at first resistant to the adaptive aids that my mom and I encouraged her to try with me when I rode. We had to prove to her that para dressage was indeed a sport and something we could work on together. Without any training in adaptive riding or classical dressage (her background was in show jumping), we were learning together.

After the failed trip to Germany, our search for a para dressage horse led us to Arizona, in the scalding heat of summer. I would not recommend the desert in summer. Ever. But there I found Chip, the best Paint horse I could ever have asked for. From Quarter Horse lineage, he was about 15.2 hands with a regal, quiet quality. Trained to give kisses, he was the goofiest gelding. He was white and chestnut, but he loved being dirty and tried time and again to turn himself full chestnut by rolling in the red dirt.

Chip was *not* a para dressage horse. But what he lacked in athleticism, he made up for in understanding and empathy. He could take a joke, and he was exactly what I needed at the time to gain confidence and integrate adaptive aids into my riding. Both my horse and I needed to learn together, just as my trainer and family and I were all learning together, venturing into uncharted territory.

My dad had a big impact on my ambition and goals as a rider. He was always very athletic and coached my brothers in their sports. Horses weren't his thing, but as a psychologist, he was interested in the mental aspect of any kind of competition. While I attribute my love of horses to my mom, my drive and determination to always do my best largely came from my dad.

He and I soon had our own pre-competition ritual. Before each show, whether we did it together in person or over the phone, we would talk about my upcoming ride, and he helped me focus and learn to work through my nerves. Looking back, I can truly see how my parents each had a significant role to play in my life—my dad, the mental side of things, and my mom, the physical. Of course, it wasn't so black and white; they shifted and took turns. But to this day, I feel they are two halves of a whole, and both an integral part of who I grew up to be. My dad was always as wholeheartedly behind my goals as I was, and his belief in my ability to accomplish big things was what kept me moving forward at full steam.

My mom and grandma measured out a ring in the grass field near the barn, and there, I practiced my first Freestyle (a dressage test to music). Despite the Michigan winter, I rode outside year-round.

The muscle tone in my hands was tight day-to-day, but my fingers would open and freeze straight out in the cold, meaning that the reins would slip out of my hands easily. I rode with a Benik brace on my left arm, which was Velcroed to the rein and the D-ring of the saddle so the arm—which I later called "Linda"—would stay down. If left untethered, the tight muscle would slowly encroach farther up my chest. Introducing additional adaptive aids, like magnetic stirrups, helped me to work with the constraints my body was placing upon me. I was in a constant battle between what my brain said I could do and my body not understanding the message.

Chip had to learn I was "attached" in a fashion to his left side and be okay with it. He could have taken advantage of me easily, but he was such a good boy. One time, we went over a jump, and unbalanced as I am, as we landed, I slid off the side of Chip. He just stopped, looked down at me, and asked with his eyes, *What are you doing down there?* Nothing seemed to faze him; he was the complete opposite of spicy Spirit, the pony I'd had before. And in that moment, I learned Chip didn't see me as different from anyone else. I was just his weird human who liked to laugh and do strange things. His acceptance taught me to embrace my body again. He forgave any miscommunication I gave with my errant limbs, which, in turn, allowed me to forgive myself. It would still be a long road ahead for me to accept myself completely, but his partnership was pivotal.

I sought out opportunities to compete, traveling to my local horse show grounds to talk with organizers and ask if they would consider offering a para dressage test during shows so I could begin to accumulate the scores I needed. Usually, organizers were understanding and would offer it for me, once I explained the situation, but it took a lot of communication and advocating for myself. My troubles at school had prepared me to speak up and ask for what I needed. Why should it be any different in the horse show world?

To this day, one of my local show grounds offers the para dressage test to competitors, and I would like to think I made a difference for a few others. My little mark on Michigan.

My goal at that point was to get my footing in the para dressage world. I would ride the test—usually the only rider onsite doing so—and send my judges' scores individually to the United States Para Equestrian Association. I wanted to qualify Chip for the National Championships and compete him against world-class para athletes around the United States. The National Championships happen together with the Paralympic selection trials. (The Paralympics, or Paralympic Games, is a series of international multisport events involving athletes with a range of disabilities that now take place following the Summer and Winter Olympic Games.) We had two years to get there, and I wanted to make it happen.

I had so much fun competing with Chip! At one show in Illinois, my mom, dad, brothers, grandparents, Aunt Lauren and Uncle Dunc, and cousin Elizabeth all came to cheer us on. We love family vacations and all stayed together at an indoor water park resort nearby. Whenever I wasn't riding, my brothers, Elizabeth, and I were in the water park in full force, acting like maniacs and living our best lives. I'm pretty sure that show was Alex and Simon's favorite of all my competitions. (While they had both tried horseback riding when they were younger, after my fall from Spirit turned me into a pretzel with my broken femur, they were traumatized, and wouldn't be caught dead on a horse.)

My favorite part of that show, however, was something quite different from the water park. It was the middle of Illinois in winter and extremely cold. Luckily, there was an indoor with a two-story indoor viewing deck. *Sweet.* But more than that, since I rode in a shorter arena than other competitors, the show organizers had Chip and I scheduled to ride early in the morning as the first to compete. Because of that, when I rode the arena was freshly dragged, which was like riding in untouched snow. There wasn't a hoofprint in sight, just the even lines where the tractor had pulled the drag behind to even out the footing. And being the first ride meant if I hustled, I could scurry up to the second-story viewing area and admire my geometry work as the lone hoofprints in the sand! It was my version of a Zen garden.

As I looked down on the arena, I remember feeling astonishment at the perfection of my circles and how far I'd come with controlling my body. Round circles are the crown jewel of any dressage test, and as I admired them that day, they gave me genuine hope for my competitive future.

Having my family at the show with me, appreciating each moment, was the icing on top of the cake—even though my Aunt Lauren was still uneasy about "all the young girls leading around their enormous horses with little to no supervision."

She was *not* a horse girl, obviously.

Unfortunately, we soon learned we couldn't afford to take Chip to the international-level competitions. The "passport" required to compete was not something we could swing, much less cross-country equine transport. Moreover, as much as I loved Chip, and as much as he was integral to the process of me regaining my confidence, he didn't have the natural movement needed to compete at an international level and justify the travel expense.

My goals were huge, but our wallets were not.

"Catch riding" was allowed in para dressage at that time, so I decided it was time to investigate that possibility.

CATCH RIDER, CATCH RIDER, MAKE ME A MATCH

Even when we first watched the para riders and horses compete at the World Equestrian Games, it was clear to my mom, and even to me, that it would take a lot of money to find a horse that could compete at the higher levels. Money my family didn't have.

I could keep training at home with Chip, but it was through the USPEA grapevine that we heard para riders could borrow horses for competition. There was an upcoming clinic in Southern California with Olympic dressage rider and coach Debbie MacDonald that I could attend if we could find the money. So my family spoke with Albion College, in Albion, Michigan, where I had competed in show jumping years before, and they held a fundraiser to help me attend the clinic and get my "official" start in para dressage. A para dressage connection then found a horse for me to borrow in California. Pegasus was a silver Knabstrupper stallion. I had never ridden a Knabstrupper, much less a stallion! What better way to give a twelve-year-old confidence?

Off we went to California! Pegasus was the fanciest horse I had ever ridden, but gentle. He had been out of work prior to me riding him, which would have made some horses silly, but he took care of me and taught me the ropes like a gentleman.

The clinic itself was challenging, with a focus on adaptive aids and how to ride eight- and ten-meter circles—often required in dressage tests. My vision issues, which cause a lack of depth perception, make riding circles hard, something I still struggle with to this day. It was frustrating, at first, but with a lot of repetition, I could eventually make a shape that resembled an actual circle! I ate it up, eager to learn more. The camaraderie among riders at the clinic was incredible. I felt *part of something.*

During the clinic, my mom, dad, and I stayed with my dad's best friend from school and his wife. I affectionately refer to them as Uncle Kurt and Aunt Liela. They have two exceptional young kids, Calvin and Phoebe, who at the time of our visit were four years old and two years old. I left their home positive I needed a little sister and begged my parents for one!

California had a special place in my heart because I'd received my CyberKnife treatment in the north and now, at the opposite end of the state, I had embarked on the next part of my journey.

Once home from California, I was determined to nail the circles we had practiced. In my previous training, I hadn't really focused on these. And of course, Chip was no Knabstrupper stallion. Bless his heart, though, he tried his best for me. He was consistent and steady; he never skipped a beat and did everything willingly. I couldn't have asked for a better horse.

When I attended my first full para dressage competition, I catch rode a Lusitano stallion named Mark. There are relatively few para dressage riders in the United States, something I'd love to change, and we are sprinkled throughout the country. We would compete wherever shows offered para dressage tests and horses were available for us to ride. This often meant traveling.

Mark was in Florida. With only one or two chances to ride him prior to the show, I didn't know him well. I clearly remember the trainer I was working with telling me not to ride to the end of the arena, because there were alligators lying in wait. Of course, the warning only made me want to see them more! (I waited until I was off my horse to go exploring, though. Why take a chance? Especially with a borrowed horse.)

Mark stepped up to the challenge with my body, deeply understanding many of my mixed signals, and just tuning out what made little sense to him.

Any *compensating* or *adaptive aids* in para dressage must be approved by the classifiers to make sure they are safe, legal, and quick-release in case of emergency. My Benik brace for my hand, which was rule compliant and something I'd competed with, was under review. While the organizers were considering it and discussing it with my mother, she suddenly noticed that I was at the other end of the arena, where I wasn't supposed to be, and my horse was rearing on his back legs.

She turned pale and came running over to us. I'd never seen her move that fast, not even when I turned into a pretzel. The trainer I was working with, however, barely blinked. "Don't worry," she said calmly. "He's trick trained." I wasn't worried. I was thrilled, loving every minute and the smile taking up my entire face. I think I even laughed aloud. I was having the time of my life. Gators and a rearing horse! How much more could a bold young rider ask for?

My mom was less impressed with Mark's performance and made me promise "not to hit that button ever again, especially during a dressage test!"

Sometimes moms are no fun at all. But my "Grammys" kept my mom and me together during stressful times. They helped find the balance between my idealism and my mom's realism.

I had both my grandmothers—or as we lovingly call them, my "Grammy Grooms"—with me at that first competition. They would go on to travel the United States with me for clinics and competitions. They were such troopers, helping in whatever way they could, not only with grooming and tacking up, but with picking up lunch and providing emotional support. My "New Grammy Nanny," my mom's mother, woke up at the crack of dawn to drive forty-five minutes from Jupiter, Florida, to Wellington on show days to support me and help me with anything I needed. My other grandmother would fly down from Michigan. They weren't horsey, but they did their best to support me.

I was so lucky to have them.

The two Grammy Grooms always had different perspectives. My New Grammy Nanny could always turn anything into a positive situation, even when I had a hard show day. One time my New Grammy Nanny was mucking a stall and got so frustrated that pieces of manure were stuck in the tines of the pitchfork that I found her handpicking out the small pieces to make sure the fork remained clean. The memory still makes me laugh.

My Grammy Grooms' very presence had a steadying effect and helped to diffuse the tension, balancing out the highs and the lows with their influence.

◇ ◇ ◇

After days of competition, the organizers' review of my Benik was finally completed. I was informed that I could compete—but my scores wouldn't count at the event if I wore the brace. It was incredibly disappointing. I needed the Benik to stabilize my hand and wrist, and the Velcro on the rein helped me keep contact with my horse's mouth. I chose to wear the brace during the review in hopes they would eventually conclude it was "breakaway" safe and allow it. Unfortunately, they did not.

After the stress of my Benik brace review, the first two days of actual competition went fine, and my scores were decent given I was on a horse I had known for only a short time. The third day was Freestyle Day, and I was so excited. I've always loved Freestyle. My Uncle Kurt does sound effects for video games, so I had asked him to create a musical soundtrack for my ride, using songs from the film *Where the Wild Things Are*. I couldn't wait for its debut.

I went down the centerline, halted and saluted to begin my test. As we hit the first corner, Mark bucked. Not just any little buck, but a full rodeo bronc situation. I somehow sat the first athletic buck, holding the reins in my right hand. Funnily, my Benik, which the organizers were so concerned wouldn't release the rein or the saddle, came off right away. Then, suddenly, I went flying and *SPLAT!* I landed hard on the ground, and everyone came running but my mother, who sauntered nonchalantly over to me as I sat there bawling (a rather different reaction than when she thought there were alligators involved!). I was checked for injuries, but because I couldn't answer them right away, through my tears and gasps for air, those who had run over to help me were terrified I was seriously hurt. Then my mom announced calmly, "Don't worry, she's just crying because she didn't get to finish her Freestyle."

She was right, darn it! I was so pissed off. My tears were those of anger, not hurt, and like any good mom, she immediately knew why I was upset and frozen on the ground.

Mark had taken my theme from *Where the Wild Things Are* to a really practical level.

I found some solace in that my Benik had, in fact, become detached, demonstrating its acceptability to the show organizers. The classifiers came up to me later and stated, "Syd, you didn't have to prove it to us."

Um, yes, I did.

I was ready for my next competition and determined to get to ride my Freestyle.

In the spring, we traveled back to California. The trip was memorable because my father took time off work and came with us, something he didn't get to do often. And because I borrowed Pegasus again for the show.

We arranged to work with Pegasus at what turned out to be his trainer's very ramshackle facility. It was less of a barn and more of a "holding area" for stallions. The trainer seemed to consider my parents to be free help, putting them to work dodging Black Widow spiders and mucking out the paddocks with the horses still inside. The muck was a foot deep—a huge, glaring, red flag.

The trainer also put me to work watching her two kids, but it wasn't much of a hardship. I was thirteen, and what teenager doesn't enjoy babysitting? I hung out with the kids in their mom's trailer, which doubled as a hoarder house. Trust me, it was better than cleaning out the pens! I had maybe two hours of practice time allotted during the two days we were there to ride Pegasus and prepare for the show.

On the first day of the competition, we had to "jog" the horses in front of judges to demonstrate they were qualified and healthy to compete. My horse wasn't waiting for me when I arrived, as he was supposed to be, and I was incredibly embarrassed in front of the judges. I left to look for my trainer and my borrowed horse at the horse trailer, and found the trainer, sitting in her truck, not grooming or preparing Pegasus like she was supposed to be doing. It was suddenly quite clear she had a drug addiction, and we realized we should have paid attention to all the red flags at her facility.

I was not dressed appropriately for grooming a horse for the jog. The jog is a chance for riders to dress nicely and parade their horses for clearance. I was wearing a fiery orange and yellow dress, with matching orange, red, and yellow hair. Now I had to rush to have Pegasus ready on time. It was the first time I was ever late to something important. I was panicked, embarrassed, sweating, and covered in dirt from my grooming effort. As if I wasn't already off to a horrible start, Pegasus jogged lame upon inspection! It was the worst-case scenario after we spent so much money and time traveling and preparing for the competition.

Pegasus had to be held for reinspection the following day, where he thankfully passed the second round.

On competition day, the trainer took so much time in the warm-up, I only had two minutes to ride Pegasus before the competition began. Because I was rushing, I didn't realize the woman had never tightened my girth, and I didn't double-check it like I should have. I rode the worst I ever had, completely unbalanced to the right as my saddle slid sideways under the watchful eye of Hope Hand, USPEA president, who was there.

I came out of the ring sheepishly, and said to her as I passed by, "Not too bad for a two-minute warm-up." I don't think she was impressed by my deflective humor.

I was embarrassed. I had scored a 55, which was *not* my best foot forward. Jonathan was there as well, seeing me ride for the first time. I could only imagine what thoughts were going through his head.

Frankly, I didn't want to know. They couldn't be worse than my own thoughts.

When we got back to the show ground barn, we found Pegasus's owner firing the drug-addled trainer. It turned into a catfight in the barn aisle, and my family was mortified. Just one aisle over from us was dressage icon and Olympian Steffen Peters. It was a memorable moment.

Luckily, Pegasus's owner found me a different trainer after the incident, a Grade V para rider, so that I could complete the show.

Talk about misadventures. With all the ups and downs to the trip, I learned a lot about "being in the moment" at a competition and how to not overthink all the bad things that can happen. Inevitably, something will go wrong. It was a very stout lesson that being prepared doesn't always matter, and you need to be ready to think on your feet. No matter what, keep going and try to make the best of it.

There was at least one big win for me at that show: I finally completed my new Freestyle!

◇ ◇ ◇

One of my later catch riding experiences was for a competition in Houston, Texas. I borrowed a large Warmblood gelding named Baron who was also being ridden by Olympic dressage rider Courtney King-Dye in her comeback to the sport after her riding accident—a horse she was schooling had tripped and she had fractured her skull and suffered a traumatic brain injury in the fall (she was not wearing a helmet at the time). I was in awe that I could be riding the same horse as one of my idols. It made me feel a connection with Courtney because we both were rebounding from a serious injury. Baron was 17.2 hands, which made the 20-meter by 40-meter ring, the size of a small dressage arena, feel even smaller. He had a big trot—in four strides it seemed I was already at the other end of the ring.

Nothing wild happened while catch riding in Texas (although I did fall while walking and get picked up by a random guy who later became my trainer at the Paralympics in Rio—more about that later); in fact, I finally just felt like part of the community. After my first two crazy experiences, maybe the third time was the charm?

Catch riding horses taught me how to think on my feet and learn a horse quickly. I've become more adjustable to a horse rather than expecting him to just perform for me. And each thing I learned on the different horses I rode in competitions came home with me to practice with my own horse, Chip.

Moreover, becoming part of the community gave me the sense of belonging I so desperately needed. Despite my rocky start in the sport, at the Texas competition I received the scores I needed to qualify for the National Championships with Chip in my first year of para dressage.

11
SUMMERS IN MAINE

When my family wasn't traveling back and forth from Michigan to California for medical procedures, or to other states for catch riding opportunities at competitions, we would drive to Maine, where my mom's parents had a house. Family vacations like these have been a big part of my life and are some of my favorite memories.

Any sane family would consider flying, but not my family! Over twenty hours in the car with three children must have been terrible (I mean, *memorable*), for my parents. We drove straight through in our fancy minivan, and my brothers and I would fight over who got to pick the movies (they had very different tastes than I did, so that was annoying). The anticipation of what awaited upon our arrival was intense.

One year, my parents decided we should go through a "drive-thru safari" in Canada (an animal park just north of Niagara Falls) on our way east. Suddenly a group of monkeys attacked our car. My brother Alex was about five years old at the time and absolutely panicked. He was terrified. Simon and I just laughed at Alex's trauma because he was always the most reactive of our family.

My parents encouraged us to play games, like the ones where we spotted license plates from various states, but we tended to be focused on the small television above us in the backseat. (What's the point of modern technology if we don't appreciate it?) I'm sure there was a lot of bickering and arguing and my parents were probably frustrated, but I remember only how excited I was to arrive at my grandparents'.

It's funny how family vacations are always stressful in the moment but leave wonderful memories behind.

We brought water with us and stopped only for food and restrooms. The water bottles left a plastic taste on the stale, home-sourced water, especially toward the end of the trip. Otherwise, we drove straight through the day and night.

Once we reached Maine, you could smell the change in the air. It was the most welcoming scent and invoked a feeling of calm and happiness. Many have tried to bottle it but with little success in capturing the pure euphoria it evokes when experiencing it in real time—a mixture of the salt from the ocean, seaweed, balsam, pine, and sunshine. There is no other smell like it. While it never seemed humid, the scent would remain always there.

To this day, when I'm around the ocean, the first thing I think of is *Maine.*

Driving through the winding, forest roads with that welcoming scent all around, we'd arrive at my grandparents' summer home in Cushing, Maine. There were two homes: the upper house, the "Hotel," and the lower house, the "Cabin," both of which were directly off the ocean. The cabin had two bedrooms and the most beautiful, reclaimed wood table that fit perfectly in with the surroundings, and a Harry-Potter-style hangout "room" the perfect size for small children, just like us. It had a tiny bed, covered with stuffed animals my New Grammy Nanny had collected over the years, a ukulele, and the smallest piano you had ever seen, fit for a doll. Of all the rooms, the hangout room was the hot spot for us kids. We would pile in and explore our musical talents… or lack thereof! Directly adjoining that was the living room, with its floor-to-ceiling windows. The sun peered in directly onto a futon that was my favorite place to sit and relax, and even nap with the warm Maine sun shining through.

The greatest part of Maine was not found inside my grandparents' house, however—it was found *outside*. The porch was spacious, looking out directly onto the ocean, complete with a picnic-style table built in, perfect for spending quality time thinking—or for messy crafts. There was a hammock in the corner of the porch, which my brothers and I found ideal for cocooning one another up and playing around.

My grandparents had four children—my mother and her three brothers—and each of them had three kids, all in a similar age range… so my grandfather had a rule that there couldn't be any "overlapping" during Maine vacations. We'd coordinate timing with my uncles so we didn't cause chaos. One year my uncle and his family were delayed leaving Maine due to a hurricane, and we had an uncharacteristic overlap that I'm sure drove my grandfather loony!

The main house had a private beach, and the tide would come in quickly. You had to be careful not to become stranded on the rocks, so you had to pay attention to your surroundings. My favorite thing to do was search for sea glass, which my New Grammy Nanny taught me all about, with blue being the most coveted color. I would use paint markers to draw on flat rocks that I collected. My grandmother was extremely artistic and creative, and it rubbed off on me. She had a craft shed filled with her projects. She'd find antiques and junk objects and make them into beautiful working clocks. She had the skill to make jewelry and metalwork. Her houses were full of art and antiques—things she found at the flea market nearby, an activity I loved to do when we visited. We would wake up at five in the morning on Flea Market Day, get bacon-egg-and-cheese croissants, and wander the stalls, talking with each vendor, who my New Grammy Nanny knew by name. She was so positive and sociable that people wanted to be near her. She always had the mentality that she would leave a person or a place better than she found it. Even in a public bathroom, she'd spend fifteen minutes cleaning it for the next person to use. In many ways, my New Grammy Nanny had a strong influence on how I socialize with others and how I see the world. I gravitated to her, and I am so happy I had the quality time with her I did, learning cribbage, doing puzzles, crafting, and of course, eating lobster.

My grandfather had a convertible at the time, and we'd whip down the roads with the top down and the wind in our hair when we needed to go "into town," the closest store being a thirty-minute drive. He loved his toys: there was also a sailboat, a motorboat, and a Zodiac inflatable off the dock. We spent so much time on the water and driving down forested roads, when I think of my summers in Maine, I only remember being completely carefree.

After my first stroke and the resulting trouble I had navigating the hills and outside areas, especially the rocks on the beach, it would have been easy to set limits for my safety. That didn't happen. My family just became more aware of me. During low tide, the dock dove sharply downward, no longer buoyed by the water. It always seemed like a fifty-fifty chance I would make it down without falling and grating my knees like parmesan. It didn't stop me from trying, and looking back, my father or someone else always seemed to "happen" to walk in front of me to make sure I didn't bite it, headfirst. (We would crab off the dock, and there was no chance I wasn't going to join in the fun!)

Despite my disabilities and our adventuring, it was surprisingly my brother Alex who was injured while at my grandparents'. We were out on an island dubbed "Otter Island," picnicking after a boat ride, and I was eating quietly with my New Grammy Nanny when suddenly my parents came running, my father carrying a sobbing Alex in his arms.

My brother had fallen while running on the rocks and gashed open his knee. We left immediately and went straight to the hospital, and he was thankfully okay.

I still find it hard to believe that I wasn't the one to get hurt in all our Maine adventures.

There is one thing that always made me nervous about Maine—the ocean. I never felt comfortable going in the water until our very last visit there. When I was twelve years old, my grandparents put the house on the market, as they had decided to retire in Florida. I forced myself to swim in the ocean off their private beach, knowing it would be my last opportunity. It was freezing, even in the summer. I'm not the person who jumps right into the deep end when it comes to cold water, which is funny because I tend to do just that when it comes to riding or horses! Instead, I slowly inched my way in, step by step, from the ladder of the dock at high tide. I knew the ocean's floor was many feet underneath me, but I still hoped to avoid any wildlife biting my toes. By the time I was fully submerged, everyone else was cold and ready to go in! But having just overcome my nerves, I didn't want to leave. It was the first time I overcame a big fear. It gave me a sense of empowerment.

Maine always had a way of giving me that gift.

In the midst of my health struggles, Maine was a carefree escape. My needs and the reality of my diagnosis had brought a lot of challenges to my young life, but our early family vacations in such a beautiful, peaceful place remained a constant source of comfort and relief. I could set aside my worries and be a kid again with both my parents and siblings in the same place. And I was lucky to spend so much quality time with my grandparents while they were alive. Our times all together as a family were few, and thus even more precious.

MENTOR

eeting Jonathan Wentz had lit a fire inside me as a rider. I wanted to bring others into the sport of para dressage. To keep the sport growing and thriving, we needed to keep attracting young riders, so they could continue the work we were beginning.

Little did I know at the time, Jonathan had been working alongside the USPEA to have para dressage incorporated in what was then called the North American Junior Young Rider Championships. At the time, all other major equestrian disciplines were represented—except for para dressage.

The first year I was involved with para, when I was twelve, Jonathan Wentz and the USPEA came to me and asked me to do a demonstration ride at the Championships. I jumped at the chance to highlight inclusion and my passion for the sport. But it was to be a

Freestyle, something I had never done with Chip, and it was to take place in the Rolex Arena at the Kentucky Horse Park, in Lexington. I had grown up watching the big international three-day event that took place there every year, and to be invited to do a demonstration within my first year of para dressage was a huge moment for me. I was over the moon!

I talked to a Freestyle designer to get some help choosing music for Chip. She sent us five or six choices to try. He really clicked with theme songs from *The Pink Panther* and *Austin Powers* with a sprinkle of *Mission Impossible*. It was a fun spy theme!

But choreographing the Freestyle itself posed a challenge. The barn where I rode didn't have a proper dressage arena, and at the time, I didn't have a place specifically measured out to work on our timing or geometry, so my mom—being the awesome "MacGyver woman" she is—set up jumping poles in a grass field in the form of a twenty by forty-foot dressage arena. The amount of preparation she put in to give me that training space was incredible, especially because she was also working as a groom at the barn to help us afford to stay in the sport. She worked her butt off with a hectic schedule, driving forty minutes each way to the barn every day, but she still fit in measuring and laying out a perfectly accurate ring so Chip and I could practice.

◇ ◇ ◇

There was so much anticipation and nerves as we practiced in advance of the demonstration. When the time came for the trip to Kentucky, approximately a five-hour drive from Michigan, Chip trailered like a champ. It was our first "long haul" with him.

Shortly after arriving at the Kentucky Horse Park and settling into the stabling, we received a message that we had to do our "soundcheck" for our demonstration. I was a first-timer—a total "newbie" to what a Freestyle soundcheck involved. I and my family assumed we needed to have my horse tacked up to enter the arena with me in order to verify the horse was comfortable with the volume of the Freestyle music over the sound system. In a nutshell, we assumed it was a bit like a dress rehearsal.

We were wrong.

We rushed to make it to the sound check on time, and I brushed, tacked up, and mounted Chip. My trainer led me across the Horse Park with the biggest grin on my face. Chip was excited, looking at everything, and fresh off the trailer! It was definitely safer with my trainer at his head, mostly because of both of our excitement level, but also because I had my eye on a few jumps set up in another arena and would have wanted to try my hand at them if given the chance!

We arrived safely at the main arena with me in the saddle, ready to do our soundcheck. I was thinking, *This is the coolest thing I have ever done in my entire life. It's our moment. Wow!*

We walked out to the center of the arena and basked in the atmosphere.

Jonathan Wentz was there, too, but something was wrong...he didn't have his horse.

Uh oh...

Suddenly, from the corner of the arena, we heard a faint, "Sydney!" and saw the flapping of arms. My trainer and I presumed a supporter was cheering that Chip and I had made it to our very first soundcheck! But soon it was made clear that Hope Hand, the president of the USPEA, was in the stands, yelling, and trying to tell us that I wasn't supposed to have my horse at soundcheck.

Should I have been embarrassed by my mistake? Perhaps. But I still felt like it was the coolest thing that had ever happened to me. A little miscommunication was not going to dull my moment. Besides, Chip and I had now made a truly unforgettable entrance to one of the most prestigious arenas in the United States!

Lesson learned: Sound checks are done on foot, not mounted. Good to know.

After a good night's rest, I was at the barn early the next day to groom Chip in preparation for our big moment. He was a Paint, and had a lot of white markings. His not-so-secret talent was finding all the poop in the stall overnight, and turning all the white hairs completely brown.

I was the first one to walk into his stall. I audibly gasped. My mom came running, thinking something must be wrong due to my audible reaction. "Mom, calm down," I reassured her, then exclaiming, "Chip doesn't have any brown spots on him anywhere!" He was miraculously clean for the first time ever. He must have known he was surrounded by much fancier horses.

It was the best surprise, especially after our misunderstanding the afternoon before. It seemed like our luck had changed.

The demonstration went incredibly well. All the hours of practice in the field my mom had marked with jump poles paid off. I did have to improvise, as often happens with horses, and luckily, because it was a Freestyle, it wasn't a big deal, and I don't think anyone noticed. My whole family was in attendance to cheer me on in what would be a pivotal event in my life. My grandfather, at the end of my ride, yelled out, "Go, Sydney!" His voice boomed and echoed throughout the arena, perhaps even the whole Horse Park. In the moment, I felt my face turn red with embarrassment, but now when I watch the video— he has since passed away—it makes me so incredibly happy that I had him with me at such an incredible moment. His pride makes me remember how lucky I've been in my family, to be surrounded by such love and support.

Appreciate the people in your life; you never know when they won't be around anymore.

When I did the demonstration at the Kentucky Horse Park, I rode directly after Jonathan. It was incredibly meaningful to ride *after* someone I looked up to so much, and the person who had not only brought me into the sport but had also become a mentor and had a vast impact on my goals and on me. We both had in the forefront of our minds that we could have an impact on future generations by bringing others into para dressage and pushing for inclusion at events like the Championships. Jonathan's mission had inspired me to follow in his footsteps, and as a new rider to the sport, I was incredibly passionate about the sense of belonging that it made me feel. I wanted to give this comfort to others who were perhaps set apart, something I was all-too-familiar with.

Riding, for me, kept me in the present moment. I didn't dwell on my disabilities, my broken bones, or the looming threat of another stroke when I was in the saddle and focused on my athletic goals. It would have been so easy to focus on the negative things in my life. I've had a lot of bad days. There were many opportunities to give up over the years, especially in my darkest times. It's infinitely harder to put one foot in front of the other while facing certain challenges, even when there might be the possibility of relief on the other side. Like anyone, I struggled some days with motivation.

Horses have always been my passion, not only riding them, but being with them. Now, setting my sights on a larger goal of one day being the level of rider Jonathan was and perhaps having his influence was giving me what I needed to keep going. As my mentor, Jonathan was a true-life example of what it meant to be a role model for others and to fight for a discipline that was all-inclusive and could give hope and promise to anyone who was "different." In him, I also found a friend, and someone who paved the way for me to push beyond my own personal goals of achievement and look outward to how what I was doing could also help others like me.

From the moment we met, I could feel the overwhelming positive energy from Jonathan Wentz. Until that day at the World Equestrian Games, I hadn't met another peer who was as passionate about horses or had achieved the kind of goals that I wanted for myself. In him, I saw myself and the potential of what could be.

I think in some ways he saw a little of himself in me as well.

We had very different lives. He was based in Texas and competing at a level that I still only dreamed of reaching. Occasionally, we'd see each other at competitions, and at those times we rode around the barns on a golf cart or hung around the stables together. He was about six years older than me, and most young men that age would not have given a pre-teen girl the time of day, but he never acted bored or annoyed. Jonathan and I matched energies, and there was something undeniable about our platonic connection. He was someone that I looked up to immensely, and he had a profound impact on my life, both in the saddle and out.

Together, Jonathan and I were forces of nature, bound together to take the sport of para dressage and use it to inspire, motivate, and include others with disabilities. It was one thing for people to look at someone and say, "Wow, what a great rider," or "I wish I could be like her one day." Our goal was to go farther and get people up out of their wheelchairs or seats and say, "*I can do this, too*, because they showed me it is possible."

Looking back on the demonstration at the Kentucky Horse Park now, I can see that it was the first big opportunity for me to help pave the way for future generations. I learned in that moment that if I kept pursuing my goals, I could do more than just win at competitions. I could have a profoundly positive impact on other people's lives *and* the world I lived in—a world that I aimed to make more welcoming for future generations.

JOURNEY

My love of riding was first put to the test when I was eight and learning and riding on borderline-crazy lesson horses. Once, during a group dressage lesson, I rode Jake, a Mustang who tended to cow kick. At the end of the arena was a pile of footing, and on this particular day, Jake zigged and I zagged—right onto the ground with a loud *pop*. I jumped right up and got on him again, riding him in both directions around the arena before dismounting and asking my mom to take me to the hospital because I knew something was wrong...very wrong.

That was my first test as a rider—falling and breaking something. Yes, the *pop* was the sound of a bone breaking (my collarbone). And even then I was incredibly determined. I knew that I had to get up, dust myself off, and get back on the pony, even if it was only for a quick lap around the arena. I didn't want Jake to think he could just ditch me or make me scared.

A collarbone isn't a glorious break. It hurts every time you breathe. Most annoyingly, while other kids broke their arms or legs and received a cool-colored cast, I had to go a different route. Rather than something neon orange, I got a lackluster sling.

It didn't really slow me down, with one exception. See, I might be a *tad* competitive. A few weeks prior to my incident with Jake, we had chosen our band instruments at school. I had always been small for my age—actually, smaller than most. So the teacher had laughed when I thought the baritone horn looked cool, and some of the other kids told me I wouldn't be able to stand up under the weight and size of it.

Challenge accepted.

Only days after my emergency room visit, I was lugging that huge piece of equipment into the band room, determined to show my teacher and classmates that they were wrong. Stubborn? Yes. But that's not always a bad thing. My stubbornness has helped me through a lot of tough times over the years.

I admit the baritone horn might have been a poor choice, though. After I broke my collarbone, it was clear that I couldn't carry the instrument with one hand. My mom got me a hand truck, and I figured out how to load the case and cart it around the school with my good side. It was my first attempt at adapting things to fit my physical limitations. I had no idea at that moment that adaptation would be my reality for the rest of my life.

Note to the reader: I have never gotten beyond the need to see any challenge as a dare to carry out. Whenever people underestimate me, it drives me harder to succeed.

My femur, which you have already heard about, was the next break, a few years later. My mom wanted me to use a cane while I healed, and I flat-out refused. Middle school is hard enough, I didn't want to feel any different than anyone else. Plus, remember, I'm stubborn.

One night I was at the movies with a friend in nearby Toledo, Ohio, which was close to my barn. My mom was working in Ann Arbor, an hour away, while I enjoyed my snacks and some tween time. As I got up to leave the theater, I pile-drove into the floor, tripping on the colorful theater carpeting and going down like a tree. *Timber!*

Wouldn't you know it, I landed on my left collarbone. Yes, the same one that I had broken coming off the Mustang a few years earlier. *Bam*—broken once again, I was in hysterical tears, lying on the floor of the movie theater.

Of course, that is a call your mom never wants to receive. She arrived as quickly as she could.

"Mom," I pleaded as she drove me to the hospital yet again. "We need to look seriously into getting me a service dog."

A service dog was the only way that I could see that I could get the "balancing help" I needed, *without* being embarrassed in front of my classmates. I already had such a hard time, feeling like I didn't belong, that I was resistant to the use of something helpful, like a cane. I strongly lobbied for a service dog, who might give me more freedom. Also, I recognized that having a dog would maybe help me be more social at school and allow me to talk to more people without the dark cloud of my disability hanging over me.

When I re-broke my collarbone at the movie theater, my left side was already being affected by the major stroke I'd suffered. My muscles constantly fired over the broken bone, and the nerves were hyper aware, causing immense and unyielding pain. And yet, the doctors sent me home without surgery.

The pain was constant, and I had trouble sleeping. About a week later, as my mom was trying to help me get more comfortable in bed, I had my second stroke, in my mom's arms. I don't remember much from the incident except that to keep me conscious, my mother poked my broken collarbone repeatedly until the ambulance arrived. She was always cool as a cucumber, even when internally she might have been panicking.

Moms, especially my mom, are strong like that.

At the hospital, an X-ray helped the doctors determine I needed surgery to install a plate for my collarbone to heal properly.

◇ ◇ ◇

I felt a service dog needed to happen to improve my quality of life, but the path to getting one was not easy. My mom applied to hundreds of organizations before she received a single acceptance. Balance and mobility dog training is highly specialized, much more so than other types of service dogs, and it takes years of training, with limited organizations that specialize in the area. But I was ravenous for my opportunity. Every day I asked my parents if they had heard a response.

At dinner one evening, my mom made the announcement: "So, there's this organization in Sterling Heights, Michigan, that may have a dog for you."

Both my dad and I exclaimed in excitement. *At last!* But he and I agreed, *as long as it's not a Standard Poodle.* We were joking, playing with the cliché that poodles are "frou-frou" and joking about a fancy-schmancy dog leading me around. My mom was utterly silent and we laughed.

I should have known then.

Finally, it came time to visit the organization that was helping me get a dog. It was an hour-long drive, and I was so excited that it felt like Christmas morning. We arrived at a house, and the dogs there lived in a pack. The woman who ran the house had a disability of her own.

We walked in and were greeted by a *ton* of dogs. The one that stuck out the most was a white dog who immediately ran over to me. I sat on the ground, and he cuddled right up to me. His name was Journey, and I at once fell in love with the two-year-old. And guess what? He was a Standard Poodle! I started laughing so hard when we were told. I had no idea a Standard Poodle could even *be* a service dog. (Journey was the first trained by the organization we were working with, and after him, they realized how smart Standard Poodles were and began to regularly incorporate them into their program.)

All summer long, the year I turned thirteen, my parents and I drove back and forth from the dog trainer's house for the sessions I was to spend together with my designated dog. Service dogs are special, and my family and I had to be trained in how to work with them, and how to interact with the public. Journey and I got to know each other over time, and I fell in love. I was so excited to bring him with me to school and have him help me talk with the other kids.

Funnily enough, Journey never actually went with me to school. By the time we were ready for him to come home and be with me full-time, I was already transitioning to online schooling. In the new scenario, having Journey made me work harder to open up my own doors and step outside my comfort zone to speak with other kids on my own. I couldn't use Journey as a crutch (no pun intended). I learned to rely on myself.

Around this time, I was receiving regular Botox injections to help the muscle tone on my left side, which had been so affected by my first stroke. It would take two hundred injections to achieve what the doctors wanted, so I had to be put under anesthesia for the duration of the treatment. After coming home from the clinic one day, I fainted. I woke up to Journey frantically licking my face and barking for help. He wasn't trained to alert others in the case of a possible emergency, but he instinctively knew what to do to help me. He was such a cool dog.

During his early training, Journey was never allowed on the furniture. But once he got to my house, the first thing I asked was for him to sleep with me in my bed. He quickly became notorious for lying on the bed with me until I fell asleep, then quietly sneaking off to his own bed on the floor. He wanted his own space, without me tossing and turning in a way that kept him awake. It was so annoying, especially considering how full of energy he was during the day. He had two full boxes of toys and would make sure biweekly to take all the toys out and give each of them enough attention. When not in harness and "working," he was such a goofball. Fetch and zoomies were a constant thing in our house.

The most "Journey moment" happened during my early training with him. We were in a Walmart with his trainer. She had me practice going into a small bathroom stall, leaving Journey outside in a "Down/Stay" position. The trainer had another dog with us, a Golden Retriever, who lay down like a rug on the ground on the command, but Journey was not about to touch a dirty bathroom floor, and hovered so that his stomach wasn't touching the ground. Talk about acting like a Poodle! Journey would do what I asked but was always perched prim and proper, watching me for my next move—a little like a creepy stalker. Or the best service dog ever! I was so lucky to have him. Not only did he help me stay balanced, but he made me laugh every day.

◇ ◇ ◇

When Journey came home for the first time, it was a huge highlight for both me and my family. We took him to the amusement park in Cedar Point, Ohio, our first venture out together. It was a big event for the new team that we were, but as you know, I love roller coasters! There is a small chance that day's activities threw my equilibrium off a bit. Will it ever stop me in the future? Nope!

About two days after our excursion to Cedar Point, I was downstairs in the basement, the house "hang out spot," where my brothers, cousin, and Journey were all vibing. When we were called to dinner and headed upstairs, I practiced my "Step, Halt, Whoa" exercise with Journey. There was no railing on the right, so I was using him to guide me and help me balance. My left foot, with the "toe drop," snagged on the stairs. I went to put weight on it without realizing it was pointed downward and lost my balance. My cousin, Gianna, was behind me and caught me as I fell backward. She probably saved me from a broken neck! My mom came running when she heard a scuffle, and told me calmly, "You're fine. Just get upstairs and we'll assess damage control."

I knew as I resumed my walk up that something wasn't right. I kept going anyway.

I made it out onto the porch and into the sunlight and looked down. My ankle was visibly ballooning and turning purple. My mom and I looked at each other.

"Uh oh," I said.

Back to the hospital, Journey alongside me. Boy, was he working hard already!

Despite the discomfort of yet another broken bone, I was excited to get my first cast *finally*. I asked for purple and lime green *with stripes*—and the doctor said yes! But then he ordered me not to ride for six to eight weeks...

In three weeks I was on (of course), walking around with no stirrup on the left to let my cast leg hang. You can't keep me off a horse!

But the break was a precursor to my next mini stroke; it was minor enough it didn't send me to the hospital but enough to reduce my balance further. I found that when my vision shifted slightly, my balance would be off—often slight migraines were my warning signs. These imbalances would lead to falls or injuries.

14
NATIONAL CHAMPIONSHIPS

All the catch riding I'd been doing was with the goal of competing my own horse, Chip, in the USEF Para Dressage National Championships in 2012. They happened to be the selection trials for the London Paralympics, as well. My aim there, however, was simply to be the youngest para dressage competitor ever and pave the way for other youth to follow in my footsteps.

Shortly before we were to trailer Chip to New Jersey for the competition, he went lame. It was a shock to everyone because he'd never been lame before. It was extremely disappointing. I was utterly devastated. It felt like the whole past year of working hard on borrowed horses had been completely for nothing. What was the use of qualifying myself for the National Championships if I couldn't compete there on my own horse like I'd always dreamed?

The world crumbled around me.

My grammy sent an email, without our knowledge, to dressage Olympian Robert Dover, whom we had seen teach at a clinic recently. The email detailed all the hard work that had culminated in the opportunity for me to compete at the National Championships—but that I was now horseless.

Robert shared the email with his followers, and Donna Ponessa, who was competing for a spot on the US Team for the London 2012 Paralympic games, reached out to my mother as a result. She offered me a horse at the barn where she trained. His name was Otto, and he had competed with her at the 2010 World Equestrian Games. Unsurprisingly, I jumped at the chance to ride the horse. Though my goal had been to ride Chip, Donna's offer meant I would still be able to compete as planned because Otto had the necessary qualifications.

I requested the help of Donna's trainer, Wes Dunham, as well. Donna was a great sport and agreed readily. I couldn't have been more grateful to train with someone of Wes's caliber and a horse with amazing talent. I am not one to pass up a golden opportunity!

I didn't ask for help when Chip went lame; instead, it was freely given through the generosity of many, and as a result, it all felt more special and life-changing. My hard work and determination would be nothing without the generosity of my family and the equestrian community who supported and developed me as a young rider. The individuals who lifted me up could very well have dismissed me and just moved on with their lives. I hope they all know how much of a difference their actions made in my life. Moreover, there actions were an expression of who *I* wanted to be as an athlete: inclusive, generous, and supportive.

I found myself traveling to New York to meet Otto and my new temporary trainer.

◇ ◇ ◇

Pulling up to the barn, we were met with a gorgeous sight. My jaw dropped. The stable was a traditionally beautiful structure with a chandelier hanging directly from the center of the main aisle and extensive pastures with a perfect manicure, rolling hills, and a vibrant green, like a golf course. It was vastly different from the "functional barns" I was used to in Michigan. I had not expected such luxury. I felt like I had leveled up. Honestly, it was like heaven.

When I met the trainer I was "borrowing," I had to laugh when I realized it was the same man who had picked me up by the scruff of my neck when I stumbled all those many months ago in Texas. It felt like fate rather than coincidence. What were the odds?

Despite the incredible atmosphere, the real draw for going to New York was to work with Wes, an incredibly no-nonsense trainer who never treated me like I had a disability. He treated me like any other rider, or perhaps was even harder on me, which made me feel incredibly strong and full of potential.

The first day of training, I learned just how big a Warmblood's trot was compared to most of the horses that I'd been riding. I would think I was doing well, and then I'd hear, "Don't dawdle around, Sydney."

I knew that working with Wes would take me to the next level and help me gain the perfectionist's eye that I'd been lacking. Because Wes wasn't afraid to push me and didn't view my disability as a positive or negative, I drove myself harder than I had previously. Within minutes of that first ride, I knew that I needed a trainer like him to help me achieve my goals.

Chip's lameness, and the disappointment, were a blessing in disguise. It set off a critical cascade of events that led me to realize I had to move away from home to be successful and excel at the sport I loved.

The competition in Gladstone, New Jersey, for the National Championships was a blur. It was a turning point in my training trajectory. I don't remember my tests or my scores, only that I somehow *qualified*. I smiled the entire ride, in a state of utter awe that I was living out my dream. And Otto was an incredibly sweet horse. (He did take a chunk out of my Uncle Tom's hand, which bled everywhere, but luckily left no lasting damage. Uncle Tom, luckily, is the most understanding and supportive uncle a girl could ask for, so he didn't hold a grudge.)

I left Gladstone now knowing that I had to go back to New York and pursue further training there. I had a taste for what it felt like to compete at a high level, ride alongside riders who were qualifying for the Paralympics, and be a peer to those who, only two years prior, I had viewed as heroes. Suddenly, a door appeared before me, and I saw a clear way to achieve my goals.

All roads led to New York.

When I returned home from New Jersey, I moved to a new dressage trainer in Michigan, but the draw of having a no-nonsense trainer like Wes who had experience with para dressage and the Paralympics remained. The problem was the distance from my home in Michigan to his base in New York.

Also, I needed a horse.

Chip was amazing, and I loved him completely, but he was not the kind of athlete I needed to be competitive at the international level. It also didn't make sense to continue to catch ride. I needed a horse that I could train with regularly and take "all the way."

In November, I traveled to Canada with Wes to look at a Warmblood and decide whether he was the right fit for me. At my level of competition, I was learning quickly that each horse was a stepping stone—each one teaches you what he can and helps bring you closer to a goal, but then, as you improve, you need to move on from that horse who helped you and look for the next one. That isn't to say horses are disposable in any way. I love horses with everything in my body; they've been a lodestone for me when my life was dark and difficult. Yet, to achieve my goals, I needed to treat my equine partners as the athletes they were, not as pets. As a horse and I improved and plateaued, our partnership was then dissolved, and I would have to search for my next partner. Finding the perfect partner for where I am *at a specific moment in time* has always been a beautiful challenge. My search for Wentworth was just such a point in time for me and contributed to my growth as an athlete and a person.

Wentworth's owner Amy had first reached out after Robert Dover had shared my story online. I went with Wes to try the prospective horse in the fall, following the National Championships.

Honestly, I have never met a horse I didn't like, but Wentworth had this goofy, lovable aura about him that made an upper-level horse that much more approachable to me. I still had my broken ankle, rocking the Joker-style cast proudly. I don't know what this horse must have thought of me, rolling up to him in a wheelchair with a strange thing on my leg. I had to ride with only a single stirrup, and my toes were exposed (and those little piggies froze in the Canadian fall weather). It was the craziest trial ride ever: Here I was on Wentworth, a horse I'd just met, with a single foot in the stirrup and a long, one-handed rein. But he took everything in stride, a smooth operator from the start—something that became readily clear when a horse broke loose outside the arena. Wentworth didn't blink, acting like, *It's chill, we got this*. He didn't care about outside stimuli, the crazy cast on my ankle, or any of that. After dismounting, I returned to my wheelchair and rolled up to him. His natural curiosity was plain, and he didn't miss a beat, putting his head directly in my lap for a nuzzle. My heart melted completely. He had to be mine.

Regularly riding a Warmblood with fancy gaits after becoming so used to my Paint with Quarter Horse gaits was a big adjustment.

As with Otto in New Jersey, my trainer had to admonish me: "Okay, Sydney—when are you actually going to trot and move him out?" But Wentworth's regular trot—not even extended!—felt huge to me, and it was a big learning curve. I had to fine-tune my riding and my feelings to really get the most out of our time together. I was putting everything on the line—my family's money, and moving away from them, to pursue a colossal dream of going to the Paralympics one day.

My move from Michigan to New York State was complicated. The initial hope was for me to keep going to school in person at home and travel to New York on the weekends, driving there and back regularly. But it took only one weekend, driving twelve hours one direction for only two days of riding, to realize that little amount of training was not going to cut it. My dad was crushed because he wanted us home, and my mom almost went crazy, trying to do the drive. We were all exhausted. It became clear quickly that I would need to move full-time to pursue training at the level I needed to achieve my goals.

My father's parents lived in North Carolina at the time, but they stepped up to help my dad, moving back to Michigan to care for my brothers while my mom and I found ourselves going east. It was a huge sacrifice for everyone, all because they believed in me.

Mom and I rented a small house near where I was training in Millbrook, New York, a beautiful town. It was a vacation cottage for some people who lived in New York City. The photos online looked amazing!

We arrived in the dead of night during a winter storm. Mom had broken her foot, slipping on a floor mat (now you know where I get my grace), and she was in a walking boot and exhausted from driving all day. Moreover, my mom hates adding more time on the road, so we hadn't eaten all day and were both incredibly hungry.

Our first impressions of what we expected to be a charming cottage were underwhelming, to say the very least. The stairs up to the house were frozen solid and falling apart—dangerous for the two of us. Mom had to get me and Journey safely inside before unloading the car. Our entire lives were in the minivan. We managed the treacherous stairs and entered the house, which was absolutely freezing. While the heat (thankfully) appeared to work just fine, the sliding door wouldn't close all the way and created a perpetual draft.

That wasn't even close to being the worst part.

The open door seemed to have been an invitation for the local wildlife to seek shelter. Almost every surface was covered in a layer of mouse droppings. It was infested.

Despite the terrible living conditions, we powered through because we knew how important it was to be there. Our future seemed shiny and new, but the reality was, my family had to sacrifice a lot for me to achieve my goals. We all just needed to keep pushing and figure out a way to make it work.

You know by now that I tend to look at the bright side of things. Perhaps in the light of day, I may have even laughed at our situation, like I do now, years later. But Mom and I were tired and hungry—not a great combination at the best of times. All we wanted was food and a clean bed.

My mom was adamant that we'd make it work. We stayed in the cottage about a month, without cable or internet, which made my online school incredibly challenging to say the least. My grandma came to check on us and was shocked and appalled by the state of our living conditions. She was absolutely stunned that we were living in a "Mouse House," wearing multiple layers and sleeping together to stay warm. (Plus, there was only one bed, so we had to share. I was the "little spoon," of course.)

I don't know if it was the mice, the cold, the single bed, or the lack of kitchen that made my grandma put her foot down.

"Screw this," Grandma said. "We're going to the Marriott."

The Marriott was glorious, like living in the lap of luxury! We stayed at the hotel for an entire month. But while there were a lot of perks, the lack of a kitchen meant we spent an incredible amount of time and money on meals.

So...we packed up everything we owned, said goodbye to the Mouse House *and* the Marriott, then moved into the Residence Inn for my next four months of training. It was a huge upgrade from the dilapidated, rodent-infested cottage, and had a small kitchenette that we could use to make food, so it was more affordable than our first hotel. But it wasn't a long-term solution.

My uncle had a friend who had a rental house in Stanfordville, a town about fifteen minutes away. We were willing to take anything—we were desperate. The home hadn't been lived in for eight years. It was built in the 1980s and my room was someone's walk-in closet, so floor-to-ceiling mirrors surrounded me. I felt like I was in a funhouse. It made mornings very interesting, to say the least!

There was reason to call our new abode Mouse House Number Two... but here it wasn't just the mice that were a problem. As humans we were now far outnumbered by the insects that had taken up residence and were aggravated by our arrival. *Spiders, everywhere.* All different kinds.

On the morning of a horse show when my grandma was staying with me because my mom was away, I woke up with a huge welt on my left arm. It was hot to the touch and had a visible ring around it. We immediately feared a tick bite and possible Lyme disease; I called my mom, who as you know by now, is never one to overreact. At first she seemed to feel the wait-and-see approach would be best. But I tried to express how hot it was to the touch. Finally, Mom said, "Go to urgent care if you're going to be that dramatic about it!"

Grandma and I went to urgent care, and while waiting there, I began to have a panic attack, hyperventilating and hallucinating that there were fairies and butterflies flying around me. As if that wasn't strange enough, I thought Journey's ears were cotton candy and began to stick them in my mouth. The horror my grandma must have felt! Because of my panic, I lost all feeling in my right hand, which perpetuated my terror as I became convinced I would lose feeling in all my upper extremities.

Honestly, I couldn't make this stuff up.

Whenever I saw new doctors, they always blamed my AVMs for any issues I might be facing, and this time was no different. The urgent care doctors were certain my hallucinations were caused by my Wyburn-Mason syndrome rather than an insect bite. No one really knows what to do with me because of my diagnosis and the experimental treatments physicians had tried in the past. Doctors who didn't know me often felt out of their depth.

As my panic abated, I grew angry, sitting in the hospital, having to deal with doctors once again when I could have been competing. Once again, my health was getting in the way of the things I wanted to do. And then I was annoyed that I had to remove my brand-new nose piercing for the MRI they insisted I have, which I fought.

This was clearly not my day.

The MRI didn't reveal much because my AVMs are tightly clustered. An angiogram was necessary to see anything important. But I was frustrated because I had gone to the doctor for a mysterious insect bite, and they instead connected my symptoms to my brain, because of my disabilities. And I was starving because my grandmother and I hadn't eaten all day. After begging hospital staff, I finally scored half a turkey sandwich—something I hate, normally, but it was my saving grace! Journey had a sensitive stomach but was allowed to eat bread for dinner because there were no other options (he thought it was glorious, too).

At midnight, they decided I needed to be transferred to the pediatric ICU in Albany, New York, which meant I had to go in an ambulance while Grammy had to drive herself, following behind. There I was seen by infectious disease specialists. Everyone was still flummoxed. Lyme disease was endemic to the area, but they were able to rule it out.

My left arm, normally tight and stiff, was loose and relaxed for the first time in years, but incredibly painful. The movement results were more improved and longer lasting than my Botox injections. It was too bad about the agonizing feeling, or I would have seen the mystery bite as a potion that could help me long term.

I stayed in Albany for weeks.

The doctors were truly baffled and gave us their best guess that I was perhaps bitten by a brown recluse spider, which although only the size of a nickel, can give bites that result in large, painful welts with a necrotic center. But it was never confirmed.

In hindsight, my next stroke occurred while I was in the hospital being treated for the bite. There was no way to truly tell whether I'd had one without an angiogram; I usually could tell because of a new loss of feeling and mobility. Coming back to riding after my hospital stay really pointed it out. I struggled to recalibrate, and my functionality was different. My balance was shifted significantly farther to the right than it had been previously, and my proprioception had altered. I felt as if my left arm was screwed on backward and like I needed to turn it around. When anyone else tried to touch it—like when it would rise up and block my view—it would lash out and try to hit others of its own volition, as if it was possessed and no longer part of my body. (This would remain the case until three years later, when I had my next stroke, and the feeling in that arm went away completely.)

As my international training truly began in New York, I was fourteen years old, halfway through my first year in high school, and completing school partially in person and partially online. It was a minor miracle because, at that time, schools were not set up for virtual learning. My school adjusted for me, but there was a learning curve for both of us, navigating how to teach, learn, study, support, and test online. Luckily, their willingness allowed me to move across the country to focus on my training and still be a student.

Splitting up my family to pursue training at a higher level was one of the most difficult things I have ever had to do. But even with a thousand miles between my mom and me, and my grandparents, brothers, and dad, we could make it work. We were incredibly lucky to have technological resources that made staying connected during the separation possible.

I used to joke that my dad really missed his calling as a long-haul trucker because he could make the drive from Michigan to New York with minimal stops and without ever stopping overnight to sleep, even when doing the drive directly following a full day of work. He and my mom were cut out of the same cloth, because she could make the drive in one sitting too. There were many miles put on our cars, traveling back and forth, and holidays became a time of coming together and being appreciative for all that we had and all the love in our family, no matter the distance between us.

I remember many instances when I missed my family deeply; it was times like that when I really had to dig in and focus on what had brought me to where I was, the overall passion I had for what I was doing, and my wish to share my mission with others. From an outside perspective, it is easy to see all that elite athletes accomplish, but what you rarely see or fully realize is the countless sacrifices made by their families, and by them, to get to that ultimate goal. My hope was that all our sacrifices would prove themselves to be worth it in the end, but of course there is never any guarantee.

WENTWORTH

16

Wentworth's arrival in New York was like Christmas morning. He was a gorgeous black Warmblood, but it wasn't his looks that mattered. His personality shone bright. His name fit him perfectly. He was part of the family the moment he arrived.

He failed turnout, however, his first week in New York. Wow, he was spunky. My trainer, Wes, rode him to prepare him for me and help wind him down from his travel south from near Ottawa, Canada. It had been a long trip, and he needed some time to settle.

Spending time with Wentworth when he first arrived was better than I ever could have imagined. He had an electric personality that was so magnetic, he just pulled you in completely. His bromance with Journey started right away. Journey would lick the inside of his nostrils, and Wentworth would nuzzle him in return. They buddied up together whenever they could, and it was the cutest thing I'd ever seen. The mutual love was clear to everyone. Journey always felt like he was bigger than he was; he was proud and strong. So, in some ways, I wonder if he imagined that he was a small horse. They got along that well.

At the time I had an Equicizer, which is a mechanical horse a rider can use for position practice and therapeutic reasons, generously donated to me by Frankie Lovato, Jr., the jockey who invented it. I named my Equicizer "Wyburn," after my diagnosis, and set him up outside Wentworth's stall. I would sit on my Equicizer, play our Freestyle music, and just hang out with him. He loved music and would bop his head along with me.

Wentworth loved any attention, but his favorite time of the day was when I would bring him a banana. Now, I hate the smell and texture of bananas with a fiery passion. I despise them. My parents would force us to eat half a banana every morning growing up, and it traumatized me. Wentworth, however, was obsessed. He was very particular about how he expected to be presented with such an offering. He was offended if I peeled it for him—he needed the complete package. And when he was done, he would lick the doorframe of his stall, as if he was instilling the scent in the wood frame and making it a "scratch and sniff" for his enjoyment later. And he didn't stop there. After licking the doorframe, he'd try to lick me with his banana-covered tongue. *Nope,* not happening! He could lick me after a sugar cube or carrot, but banana-breath? Not a chance.

Wentworth arrived in the winter, and by summer we were competing at HITS Saugerties, a showground close by. We were new to each other, but he took everything in stride. HITS horse shows can be chaotic: there was always a lot going on in the background with multiple rings, golf carts, bikes, motor scooters, dogs, and of course, all the other horses and riders.

One of our very first shows together, my vision shifted without my knowing. I rode down the centerline to salute the judge and began my test as I normally did, not realizing what had happened. When I finished, I rode out with a gigantic smile on my face.

Wes looked at me, and said, "Are you okay, Sydney?"

"Why?" I replied enthusiastically. "That was awesome, right?"

"Well," he said. "It would have been, except you rode your entire test five meters off to the right."

This was the first of many instances when my vision affected my rides.

My depth perception was shot, and I had no idea. Luckily, I was allowed to ride the test again and cancel out my initial scores. As I did my final salute, the award ceremony at the nearby jumper ring began and loud music started to play. It was loud, and frankly a little alarming. Wentworth's head shot up, but he kept his equilibrium. He always had my back and took care of me every ride, but he was also a little bit lazy. Spooking would have been extra effort, and Wentworth never did more than he had to. He had to be convinced to give his all!

Wentworth was what I needed to build my confidence and learn how to handle a Warmblood. We rode out on the roads, over hills, and winding across a beautiful upstate New York landscape to mix up our arena training. Because my horse was a "more whoa than go" type, we usually ended up behind the group on a trail ride, quietly enjoying the scenery. Sometimes, Wentworth couldn't be persuaded to even try to keep up with his friends.

He was a spectacular horse, though. We trained with Wes six days a week. I was simultaneously doing physical therapy with my left ankle (following the break on the stairwell) and working with a personal trainer three days a week, and then also strength training on my own.

◇ ◇ ◇

Approximately nine months after he arrived, in the summer of 2013, Wentworth played a little too hard in the paddock and broke his coffin bone, the bottommost bone in the leg (encased in the hoof). The injury required six months' strict stall rest. My (basically) new horse was out of training and competition for the foreseeable future.

It was incredibly disappointing. My family had invested so much money in this horse, and so much time had been put into training, with our scores just starting to go up with each competition. Our goal when buying Wentworth was always for us to compete at the 2014 World Equestrian Games, but life kept throwing hurdles in our way. Wentworth's injury was catastrophic for us. (I have to note here that to the time of writing, I've never competed with my own horse at the five-star level. My family and friends and trainer had a running joke, years later, that Wentworth had a secret contract that indicated he would only compete domestically and never travel on a plane.)

We began urgently hunting for a horse that I could compete while Wentworth healed. We contacted many people, including the chef d'équipe (coach) for the WEG team to see if he had any horses available. Wes spoke with the owner of a horse named NTEC Cuplee at my barn; she agreed that he might be a good fit for me. He was only six years old and 17.2 hands, which meant I needed a four-step mounting block (that means big!). He was also not the easiest horse by any means. He had his "baby brain" moments from time to time, and I had to quickly learn to be forgiving because we were learning together. My previous years of catch riding helped me as I applied everything I'd learned on this young horse.

I rode Cuplee at the Saratoga showgrounds shortly after starting with him. While riding my Freestyle (why is it always my Freestyle?) a huge, unidentified insect landed on Cuplee's butt. I'm talking a *bird-sized* bug. Cuplee bucked, and my left foot came flying out of the stirrup, so I had to complete my test with only a single stirrup for stability. I'm already off balance, so why not add a little spice?

As if that wasn't enough, a group of motorcycles came barreling up the road nearby, and the young horse spooked in a major way. There was a big difference between my inexperienced mount and calm, collected Wentworth! But I stuck to that saddle like glue and am extremely proud that I stayed on. Cuplee was actually a really giving horse—after all, we had only been together a short time, and he tried his best for me. I couldn't ask for more and was so grateful just to be there.

Kai Handt, the chef d'équipe of the Para Dressage Team, also had a horse for me in Texas, where he based his training, that he thought might be a good candidate to compete alongside Cuplee. Willi Wesley was an older and more seasoned gelding than Cuplee, so my mom and I traveled back and forth on good ol' Spirit Airlines so I could train with Kai and Willi Wesley. The Spirit terminal at the LaGuardia and Newark airports were a bit outdated, and some of our flights were a little scary, but we were able to alternate schooling one week in Texas, then one week in New York.

While the opportunity was bittersweet, since I couldn't compete with my own horse once again, I did get to ride two distinctly different horses. More than that, Dallas, Texas, was where Jonathan's family was based.

Tragically, the world had lost Jonathan in September of 2012, right after the London Paralympics, where he had successfully competed as the highest-scoring rider for the United States in all dressage competition, Olympic and Paralympic alike. He was only twenty-one years old when he passed.

I felt his loss greatly; he had been both a mentor and a friend. It hit me so deeply that, even today, I still haven't recovered from the news that he was gone. It didn't seem possible that he was no longer with us, no longer laughing by my side, no longer encouraging me to chase my dreams. He helped me learn to see myself as more than just someone with a disability.

I stayed at his family's home while I trained in Texas. It allowed me to experience what his life had been like behind the scenes. His mom Tina and I became closer, and she took me to his favorite restaurants. I rode at his home barn and with Kai, who had been his coach. It made me feel much closer to him at a time when I needed it.

School had taken a backseat to my travel and training. High school was not my favorite thing, to begin with, and I was a perfectionist and wanted to get great grades, but the online study program wasn't set up for me to be as successful as I would have liked. Plus, I had a lot on my plate. I wanted to give my all to my riding and dressage training. School was an added stressor, and because I didn't have any online deadlines, I kept pushing my studies off. I was drowning, leaving everything to the end of the trimester and finding myself overwhelmed. Somehow, miraculously, I didn't fail out. (Later, college was different for me, with rigid schedules and deadlines in a true, online degree program, and I excelled.)

◇ ◇ ◇

I have to keep moving forward in the face of adversity. I try to always look at it as, "Okay, what now?" It doesn't help me to dwell on the difficult challenges. And life *does* have its challenges. Optimism has been my best friend. I also have a team behind me, supporting me and helping me when things are tough. I have never felt alone because of those around me who want to see me shine.

Nothing in life ever really goes as planned, but I keep pushing at it. Somehow, in the end, it all works out for the best.

GET READY, WEG, HERE I COME

My time in Texas training with Kai Handt and Willi Wesley was extremely important to me. It was a beautiful thing, my finding them, given Kai had been Jonathan's trainer. Being in Kai's barn meant that I was able to visit Jonathan's horse, Richter Scale, and spoil him with apples and carrots.

Richter Scale was a "wooly mammoth" of a horse. He was immense, with hooves the size of dinner plates, and a head to match. I vividly remember how humongous his head was—and that he somehow pulled it off. In the show ring he had been incredibly well-matched with Jonathan and his long legs. They had been sort of the "misfits" of para dressage, with Jonathan's big personality and his unconventional horse. While I had ridden bigger horses, Richter was so incredibly powerful, I fawned all over him.

My grief was so fresh when we were in Texas, and so was his family's.

My mother and Jonathan's mother became closer with each of our visits. They would stay up late into the night, chatting. Our mothers were uniquely similar, in that they both knew what it was to have a child with different needs. Not only that, but they were united in the incredible sacrifice it took to try to make their children's dreams into reality. It was a life that could be both stressful and lonely.

That our mothers found each other and became listening ears for each other, and supportive friends when things got hard, became yet another blessing from my relationship with my mentor. Even in his absence, his memory united others and helped them build strong connections.

The fact that I was surrounded by people who made me believe in myself and that my goals were possible convinced me that somehow, in some way, Jonathan had a hand in it and had guided us all together. And while I was devastated that my own horse was lame and unable to compete, Wentworth's injury created an opportunity I may not have had otherwise, both in my career and in my personal life.

◇ ◇ ◇

I should mention one important thing here: I qualified for the 2014 World Equestrian Games!

No big deal, just an incredible time in my life.

The selection trials took place at the historic Hamilton Farm in Gladstone, New Jersey—home of the United States Equestrian Team (USET)—in June 2014. It was a beautiful venue. I was riding around on my scooter when they announced the Para Dressage Team, and I remember clearly there being some confusion, and me thinking, *I didn't get it.* The pure adrenaline that rolled through my body when I found out I *did*, in fact, make the Team—a goal I'd had since that trip to WEG in Kentucky four years before—was intense. It was electrifying— butterflies that made all the difficulties worthwhile.

The moment was somewhat numbed by the drug test I was asked to take immediately after the announcement.

"Hey, congratulations on making the Team! Now go pee in a cup."

We had to collect our own urine sample under observation. Let me tell you, it was a little difficult with only one working hand. It was not an easy feat to maneuver "Cup A" and "Cup B," and their lids, which had to lock perfectly. There was a script I had to follow to the letter to adhere to the guidelines. Luckily, they allowed me assistance—otherwise there would have been a mess everywhere!

Team riders were told to keep the list of who made it under wraps until the official announcement by the United States Equestrian Federation on the fifth of July. It was extremely difficult for me to not shout the news to the rooftops. I am an "open book" as a person, so the secret was an utter challenge.

I was also told I needed to kick things up a notch because the World Equestrian Games were in August—only a few weeks away.

Both Cuplee and Willi Wesley were extremely talented, but more than that, they were accepting. They understood me.

Yet, although they were similar in these ways, they were also incredibly different.

Cuplee was young and green, but big-bodied—the largest horse I'd ridden to date. He was an elegant mover, interspersed with periodic moments of "baby brain." Everything we did together was a learning process. Moreover, he had never had a rider like me with my disabilities and adaptations. He had kind eyes, and his energy was Zen as he focused on me.

By contrast, Willi Wesley was a seasoned professional. I'd seen Kai compete him in the Grand Prix at a CDI where I'd been catch riding the year before. ("CDI" stands for *Concours de Dressage International,* which is just an international dressage event recognized by the FEI.) The horse was stunning, and I was humbled and astonished that Kai would view me in all my fifteen-year-old glory to be good enough to ride him. Willi had more experience in competition than I did. He was serious about his job and gave his all. He loved being the center of attention and it showed. His trot was so big, I would choose to post my trot in my tests because it felt like I was floating in the air. What prepared me for riding a horse of his level was the year of catch riding so many horses. I had learned to improvise and think on the fly, which enabled me to build a relationship with two very different horses and to do it quickly. My experience had created an adjustable mindset so that I could stay in the moment and be prepared for any situation.

Our travel to and from Texas was an adventure of its own. My mother was an intense flyer. It took us approximately an hour and a half to get to the New York area airports, which always seemed to be under construction, and her need to be there, at minimum, two hours before the flight—after all, we had a wheelchair and a service dog, which could complicate things— made for a lot of anxiety. You would think we'd have been better at traveling since we'd had to do it so often, but it was always the one thing that seemed to break my mom's calm.

I spent our car rides giving my mother directions, and if I missed a turn, the intensity in the car would go into overdrive! But the worst thing that could happen was missing a flight, and being with someone who had a disability often did make things move more slowly. For affordability, we'd choose off-airport parking, and we had to schlep with our suitcases, a wheelchair, a service dog, a cane, and adapted dressage whip onto a shuttle. Load, unload...traveling with me was a lot of work, I admit it. And we had to do all this multiple times a month! Thankfully, we had direct flights, or else I'm sure my mom would have been a sobbing mess. I'm sure my constant chatter and questions didn't help her nerves.

I owe my mom a lot of apologies!

My service dog, Journey, was a champion. He'd been on airplanes in training but never actually flown—but he never had a problem with us, sleeping for most of the flight and taking everything in stride.

(This was something that would come in handy later, when we had international flights.)

I used the plane rides to shift my mindset into one that would work with the horse I was traveling to ride. The mental aspect of equestrian sport is often undervalued and was something I was still learning at the time. While training in New York and Texas meant two different horses, it helped that both Wes and Kai had similar training styles. It made it easier for me to connect the dots because it kept the voice in my head consistent.

I competed both horses until the selection for the World Equestrian Games. I was secretly hoping I'd qualify with Cuplee because he was local, and it would make things much easier for me and my family. But when was my life ever easy? So, it was no real surprise when the selectors chose Willi Wesley as my partner. Looking back, I agree it was the right move to have an older, more seasoned horse under me for my first Games. (Cuplee was named my backup horse, in case of emergency.)

With Willi as my partner, I spent the bulk of the summer in Texas to get ready for our event. Summers in Texas are no joke. I lost an incredible amount of weight through sweat alone. By the time we'd tacked up, I'd be drenched through my clothing. Yet, I powered through, even while riding in the middle of the day, at the mercy of Kai's training schedule. Each ride was followed by strength training at the gym, and occasionally, we'd visit the community pool for a nice dip to beat the heat.

I now had even more clarity in terms of what I was training for. The set date for the World Equestrian Games gave me a goal, and I loved my teammates. (It helped that all of us were already friends, leading up to the event.) I never felt outside pressure. Instead, I focused on each day, one at a time. I had to ride the horse I was on at the moment. I felt prepared, despite it being my first WEG and first ever international competition.

Normandy, France, here I come!

Our Para Dressage Team was spread out across the United States, with riders in Texas, California, New York, and Pennsylvania. There were challenges to living across the country from my teammates. Still, I was no stranger to travel, and there was nothing that was going to dampen my excitement.

That said, it was a long, hard adjustment. The weather in Texas was a factor, certainly. Emotionally, our time in Texas was charged because I felt so much closer to Jonathan, seeing his horse every day and training under Kai, who had shaped Jonathan into who he was as a rider. There were good and bad days, just like anything. My body always seemed to want to make things more challenging. I was constantly fighting with myself. Kai was a no-nonsense trainer who had experience with para riders, and I loved his dry sense of humor and ability to see past my limitations and try to forge me into the best athlete I could be.

There were times I came home crying, frustrated with myself at not being able to perform how I knew I could. Although driven to achieve my goals, I was still a teenager with all those hormones bouncing around, and the often-fragile mindset that could come with it. When I was in the saddle, I had many trainers' voices in my head. Every trainer that I'd worked with over the years had left a mark, and they all came with me into the arena. At this point, I was mentally a hot mess. There was a huge mental aspect missing in my training and preparation. I had big goals and aspirations, but I didn't have the mental resources to make it happen. I was new to the sport and didn't realize that physical skill was only a small part of the whole.

But that hot, Texas summer made me tough as nails, teaching me to take in what I needed to be my best and how to become moldable to other training styles, rather than fighting against them. I became more critical of my own riding, which allowed me to think more in the moment and be on my toes in the show ring. I became a perfectionist on horseback, something that is needed in the sport of dressage.

I was determined to live my life to the fullest and achieve goals only a handful of adults would ever realize. The pressure I put on myself was immense, but I was so focused, I didn't see what I was missing at the time. How could I, really? I was a child. Yes, I had grown up quickly, but it's easier to see the holes in my training and education from my perspective now.

I learned later, after working with a sport psychologist, to visualize my rides in my head right before my test. After WEG, I actually began to draw out my test on paper with cues to help me focus, and I continued to do this for years—almost to my own downfall because I would focus so much on my cues or plans that I would forget to ride the horse I was on. I had a real fear of making a mistake, turning the wrong way, or riding off course.

The biggest thing I learned through my experiences preparing for and riding at WEG was to not focus on the negative, as that only led to riding with frustration or anger. Focusing on the *good* parts of a ride, where things felt smooth and like we were moving with a nice pace, helped me to ride with happiness. Everything flowed better once I changed my mindset. I had been listening to the negative voices for a long time, and it never helped my ride and had nothing to do with the horse. If, however, I stayed in the moment, and was positive, it showed in my riding and made me a better partner for my horse.

A few weeks before WEG, all the riders on my team traveled to the United States Equestrian Team headquarters in Gladstone, New Jersey, for a week-long training camp. The four Team members, as well as our individual para rider, all came together for the first time. The goal was to make sure we were capable of solid rides, the horses were sound and ready for travel, and we could quarantine together.

Willi Wesley and another teammate's horse traveled together to New Jersey from Texas. Luckily, our horses traveled well and had no issues with their long-distance ride across the country. That week we focused on light riding, practicing our tests but not pushing our horses, and making sure they were stretched and comfortable prior to the upcoming trip *across the ocean* to Normandy in France. Time passed in a whirlwind of excitement and activity. Before we knew it, it was time to leave.

WEG 2014 was my first time experiencing what it was like to transport horses on airplanes. The Team horses traveled on the same flight as us out of John F. Kennedy International Airport. The front half of our plane was traditional seating for people, while the back was cargo, with room for the horses. It was surreal, looking out the window and seeing our horses in their travel crates being lifted onto the back of the plane. More incredibly, our flight was an open, commercial flight, and the other ticket holders had no idea there were going to be horses on board!

Although Wentworth couldn't be my horse for WEG, we had contacted his former owner, Amy, to see if she'd be willing to be our groom for the games. It was such an amazing opportunity to spend more time with her, and she became a great friend as I witnessed her fantastic care of Willi Westley. It was an incredible experience for her, also— she was chosen to sit in the back of the plane with the horses and help the flight veterinarian, if needed.

We flew into Frankfurt, Germany, then took a high-speed train to Aachen from there. This was our week of prep before completing our travel to Normandy and the competition. Somehow Kai, who was a *bereiter* (licensed instructor) in Germany, finagled it so we could stay in an incredible five-star hotel. The beds with their down comforters were like sleeping on clouds. Mornings were a cappuccino with a rock candy stirrer. I felt like a queen. I had never experienced Europe like that, even though I had been to Germany during that previous horse-shopping excursion.

At this point, reality kicked in, and the pressure started to take hold. *I was in Europe about to compete at the World Equestrian Games on behalf of my country.* But my practice rides were disappointing. My body was not doing what I wanted it to do.

I felt like a stranger in my own skin. I knew what I had to do, but it wouldn't translate from my brain to my body. Looking back, I think the stress to perform created problems for me, rather than my health issues. I was only sixteen years old at the time, competing at the top level of international sport, and the stakes were high.

Despite my disappointing rides, I felt incredibly lucky to be there as part of such an amazing team. That gratitude helped me focus until I finally felt ready to ride down the centerline. Things began to click into place for me by the end of training camp.

When we headed to Normandy, where the Games were being held, there was record rainfall and mud everywhere. My wheelchair kept getting stuck, and my pristine white Poodle was, well, not white. And there was a problem with our accreditations. Security refused to allow my service dog access. We reasoned with them, explaining that he was needed for my vision and mobility. He was clearly marked with his harness and his paperwork was ready to go and all in order.

When the security suddenly called me into their main office, we assumed there was going to be a huge problem. We were not off to a great start. But then one of the officers came out, holding official event credentials, which he presented to Journey as if my dog was being knighted! Of course, the gentleman Poodle that he was, Journey accepted the honor proudly and graciously. It was the greatest moment in the history of the World Equestrian Games. He was the only service dog to get accredited to go into a five-star barn. It broke the internet! Journey was officially more famous than me. If I hadn't loved him so much, I would have been slightly jealous.

My dog loved every minute of the attention he received after that. The French newspapers wrote articles about him, and he became "The Story" from that year's WEG. More than that, it was a historic moment for service dogs in general, as he helped open doors for animals of his training to be accepted at major sporting events. It raised awareness of and accessibility for other dogs in his line of work.

Journey's experience was my first glimpse of our potential to make an enormous difference in the world. Journey became an icon through his WEG fame. His confidence and radiant energy drew people to him, and his seriousness in relation to his work demonstrated how important his kind of training was for people with disabilities. When we were invited to be interviewed on FEI Television, I believe one hundred percent that they invited me because of my dog, and I wouldn't have been there if it wasn't for him. He opened doors for me in more ways than we ever dreamed.

◇ ◇ ◇

I was the youngest rider of the *entire* World Equestrian Games that year—that means *all* the disciplines. My youth didn't really matter, but my inexperience definitely impacted my performance.

The horses were incredibly spooky because the arena had branding that was unfamiliar and slightly scary for them. That was fun to ride through! As a visually impaired rider, I found it a significant challenge. In every arena I rode in, I had to identify points of reference so I could ride an accurate test. But as you know from stories I've already shared, sometimes my eyes played tricks on me. Imagine living in a funhouse where you can't trust what your eyes are telling you and they affect your depth perception. I had to rely on my understanding of the arena and how it was set up more than my eyes, which was a difficulty. Each arena is different depending on the footing, the lighting, and the spectator seating, so this presented a new hurdle, in addition to the physical test of riding.

In my first test at WEG, the bell rang, signaling I should enter the ring, and I jumped into action, almost bowling over Wes. It was like my eventing experience suddenly kicked in and I jumpstarted. I was on the centerline before I realized that I'd almost run my trainer over.

I was actually thrilled with my test. After I tried to bowl with my trainer, of course.

My ride wasn't perfect. It gave me a reason to push harder and do better the next time. The walk work wasn't as forward or flowing as I would have preferred—I held Willi back a little too much—but our trot was great. I looked at our test as something to build on.

I got to ride two tests, but because I finished outside the top eight, I was done for the Games and wouldn't continue any further. I was disappointed I couldn't ride my Freestyle. (Fun fact: At the time of writing this book, I have yet to ride a Freestyle at an international competition. It's my white whale and "must-do" I am pursuing with dedication.)

Wes was on hand as my personal trainer, but Kai, as the chef d'équipe for the US Team, was also there. There was a feeling of being torn between the two when they would each give me advice. It was challenging because I didn't want to hurt anyone's feelings, and I did *not* wish to stir up controversy. I wanted to be the best student I could for *both* trainers and make each of them feel like I was listening. It was a unique position for me to be in, and it complicated matters, especially when their opinions differed. Looking back and with the experience I have now, it would have been helpful to have a sport psychologist to help me navigate the situation and be more assertive. I underestimated just how much show nerves could affect me and my performance.

Although overall the Team performed well, we did not get the results we were hoping for or would have liked. That didn't keep us from enjoying our time in France and the experiences we were having. We spent a lot of time together in the barn and at meals.

One meal was particularly memorable. It was very late one evening, and all of us staying at the team hotel were tired and starving and wanted dinner. Looking at the menu, we read what we *thought* was andouille sausage. It sounded like something that would hit the spot perfectly, so the entire team ordered it.

We should have known something was up when the waiter raised his eyebrows at our order and laughed under his breath.

Out he came out with six plates of sausages, which smelled incredibly fragrant and looked lumpy. I tried to cut my sausage into a bite-size piece, but the casing spilled open, and what was inside was not ground in the way we are familiar in the United States. You could see *everything* that you never wanted to! Our Team veterinarian started pointing out the various innards in our "andouille sausage"—and made an attempt to eat it, anyway.

Everyone except our vet skipped dinner and ate only chocolate mousse.

◇ ◇ ◇

One of the highlights of my trip to France was not the Games themselves, but the fact that my family came to cheer me on. My father, brothers, and grandparents from both sides of my family all flew across the Atlantic to see me compete in Normandy. It meant the world to me. Plus they got to go sight-seeing while I was training and preparing for competition. It was an amazing experience for them, and they deserved it because if it wasn't for them and all their love, support, and sacrifices, I wouldn't have been able to achieve the dream. It was only right that we shared the spoils together. It was insanely special.

After I was done competing, I stayed and cheered my teammates on, enjoying the entire World Equestrian Games. I then joined the family sightseeing, going to Paris for a week and spending quality time together in such a beautiful city. Cobblestone streets are not exactly wheelchair friendly, so we had some hairy moments, but we got to visit the Eiffel Tower, the Louvre and other museums, and eat the most delectable food. It was fun to be an American in Paris, and the cherry on top of the WEG sundae.

Journey had been the superstar of the Games, according to the press, but he was not sure about Paris. Our hotel didn't have any parks nearby, so he had to use a street alleyway as his restroom, and he did not love the "splashback" that occurred.

Like most things in my life, there couldn't be good without a little chaos.

The emotions I felt after the World Equestrian Games were significant. I had worked so hard for many years with this one event as my focus. It had been my sole, driving goal. After my rides were done, after I was done cheering on my country, I sat in my hotel room with my dad and broke down, crying. The letdown one can sometimes experience after a major life event was something I had never experienced, nor was it something I predicted. I had no idea what my next step would be. For the first time, I didn't know where I was going, and it scared me.

18
AGAINST ALL ODDS

The email from the United States Equestrian Federation informing me I had won Junior Equestrian of the Year for the 2014 US Equestrian Pegasus Awards was quite unexpected. My goal had been to be a voice for the underdog and show people how capable a disabled rider could be. Making the Team for the World Equestrian Games was a huge milestone in the pursuit of that goal. Riding in Normandy had been an honor. To come home, dealing with all the feelings of post-competition letdown, and receive such an award helped me regain my focus.

The awards gala was held right in the heart of horse country, in downtown Lexington, Kentucky, that October. It was close enough for my extended family to come and cheer me on. What was especially neat about the ceremony was that my brother Alex, who is pretty shy, wheeled me onto the stage to receive the award. Having him be willing to come onstage and do the photo ops and be an active part of the ceremony was incredibly special. He had always faded into the background whenever possible, and both my brothers had spent so much time traveling and attending my competitions over the years, I felt it was only right they got to share in the limelight. After all, they had sacrificed a lot for me to achieve my dreams. It stood to reason they should be recognized for everything they had contributed to my success.

There were so many wonderful equestrians present at the awards, including Olympic show jumper and living legend Beezie Madden, who won Equestrian of the Year. I had met Beezie in passing before, but at the gala I was able to personally congratulate her on her award, which was incredibly cool. I felt so honored to be amongst individuals I counted as celebrities, even if I didn't feel like I was an athlete on the same level. Imposter syndrome can catch us all, and I was by no means immune to it.

My goal was always to get the best results at WEG: win the gold. Beyond that, my motivation was to change people's perspectives for the better and show them anything is possible when you work hard enough. The awards after WEG were reassurance that I was on the right track. These wins helped me push through the harder, disappointing days. The equestrian community rallied around me and helped lift me up.

Returning from France to be notified I had not only won the Pegasus Award, but then miraculously, something even bigger, meant it was a whirlwind few months!

Luckily, I thrive in chaos.

◇ ◇ ◇

I was in Michigan, at home with my family, when I got the surprise phone call. I happened to be putting on my makeup at the time, as I listened to an official-sounding voice inform me I had won the FEI Against All Odds Award.

There went my makeup.

Tears poured down my face as I ran downstairs to tell my family. Of course, I shouldn't have been running anywhere, much less down the stairs. I didn't have the best track record.

I raced into the living room and shouted, "Mom, I won the FEI award and it's going to be in Baku, Azerbaijan! Where in the heck is that?"

I had no idea at the time, but after a quick Google search, I was even *more* excited.

Each major "game cycle," approximately every two years, the FEI recognizes a small number of people, including the recipient of the Against All Odds Award. It's a huge honor. The Against All Odds awards celebrates someone who faces adversity to accomplish a specific goal with courage. Someone must nominate you (self-nominations don't count), and then online voting dictates the winner. My WEG groom, Amy, had nominated me without my knowledge. And since I was still a minor, my mom was running my social media, so I was completely blindsided by the honor—in the best of ways!

It was the most special phone call I've ever received. It was surreal.

I began researching Baku immediately, the capital of this country I was going to get to visit on the Caspian Sea. It reminded me of a mini Dubai—at least, what I knew of it. The country was tiny, and most people would never have the chance to travel there, so I felt extremely fortunate to get to experience it firsthand.

When we received the itinerary for the awards, it was chock full of events and needed no fewer than *three* cocktail dresses. Three! And then a "black-tie" gown.

This was completely outside my usual clothing choices.

When I told my Uncle Tom and Uncle Martin I needed cocktail dresses and an evening gown for my upcoming award ceremony, they jumped at the chance to take me shopping. Thankfully they had a lot of fashion sense. (The dresses we chose also had to be able to keep up with my moves on the dance floor, because I'm an unstoppable force!) My mom and I would have easily shopped off the racks at the local Macy's, but my uncles had other ideas.

Luckily, it was a quick one-and-a-half-hour drive to Chelsea, the neighborhood in New York City where my uncles lived. Any day off from training that summer, Mom and I would drive into the city to try dresses. My Uncle Tom worked at the Bergdorf Goodman Salon, and the store also had women's evening wear, so naturally we went there first to look for the evening gown. And the first dress was the one! It was floor-length with a sweetheart neckline and beaded, hand-stitched fabric. It was stunning: perfect fit, perfect everything.

Except for one thing—the price.

We left the gown behind and went to lunch. I tried to stop thinking about the dress; I tried to stop justifying the price. *I could wear it to prom. I could even wear it to my funeral!* There were so many events that I could wear it to. After lunch we had a lot of fun dress hunting at every large department store in the city. I found some amazing cocktail dresses, but no evening gown was better than the first.

We went at least four more times to the city in search of a gown for Azerbaijan. Uncle Tom offered his employee discount to help me purchase the first gown. I really won the "Uncle Lottery"! I was so grateful—the dress was just as beautiful as I remembered and would be tailored to fit me even more perfectly. It was a true Cinderella moment. I felt like a princess. I had never gotten dressed up or gone to school dances because riding was always my focus. My priority had never been personal appearance—the most dressed up I ever got was for trot-ups at my competitions.

The FEI flew me and my parents on Azerbaijan Airlines. I loved that my dad could come along and experience the trip with us. Mom and I flew Business Class thanks to Journey, but Dad was on his own in Economy.

On the day of our departing flight, we were held up leaving Millbrook and sat in the worst traffic in New York. As you already know, my mom is an anxious traveler, and my dad started teasing her to try and lift the mood. Well, Mom broke down sobbing, terrified we were going to miss the flight. Dad also thought it was an appropriate moment to let me know my great-grandma had died. She was ninety-seven, so it wasn't a shock, but still—it was like the car ride from hell.

My dad is not exactly known for his timing.

Thankfully, we made it to the airport without any more drama or surprise revelations. The airline was obscure, but we found it. When we checked in and handed the airline attendants Journey's paperwork, they asked if we had a muzzle for him. Of course, I said, "No, he's a service dog." That unfortunately seemed to confuse the staff at the desk, and they had to have a sidebar conversation. We had several tense moments before they finally allowed us to continue through security and board the plane.

Our Business Class seats reclined into beds, and the flight attendants fed us nonstop. When I was presented with a dessert tray, I chose one dessert, but apparently, they were actually giving me the entire tray! *Don't mind if I do!* Finally, my mom had to stop me. "Syd," she warned, "you have to stop or you won't fit in your dress!"

Calories don't really count at elevation, right?

The flight was twenty-two hours. Journey slept the entire time, and some of the flight attendants didn't even realize there was a dog on the plane!

Upon arrival, there was an eight-hour time difference that we had to assimilate to. We were travel weary, and we were excited to get to our hotel so we could sleep and freshen up. But there was a camera crew waiting for us when we stepped off the plane. Not ideal when you've been sitting in your own travel dust for a day. It was a big hullabaloo!

The airport was beautifully clean and futuristic looking. It reminded me of something one might see in the Capitol from *The Hunger Games.* It felt odd, however, that the space was largely empty except for us, the camera crew, and some airport workers.

We were told Journey was the first service dog to be in the country. We found out later most dogs in Azerbaijan were used as guardians or protectors and thus had reputations for being aggressive. It was a big surprise for people to see my dog, with his strong work ethic and impeccable manners, by my side. We were asked often, "Will he bite?"

Limos were waiting for us at the exit. Journey and I had one just for us, and my parents were put in a separate limo. It never occurred to me to be worried or anxious—in fact, I felt like a celebrity, getting my own car.

Mom and Dad and I were aware we would be staying in a famous hotel, but we didn't research it in advance, as we didn't want to ruin the surprise of experiencing it live for the first time. We drove through city streets, lined with fancy buildings, walls, and construction everywhere. The architecture was stunning—one building looked like a rolling carpet! Then we approached our hotel, which was housed in the famous Baku Flame Towers, a series of three buildings designed to look like flames, with exteriors covered in dramatic LED lights. In the evening, the towers actually appeared to "flicker," becoming a beacon across the city.

By the time we arrived at the hotel, we'd been traveling for twenty-six hours without stopping, and poor Journey *really* had to go to the bathroom. But we were swept away by the concierge, who escorted us to our suite on the twenty-eighth floor and gave us a tour. The stunning views through floor-to-ceiling windows and the ultra-sleek, modern design was nothing less than incredible. The bathroom mirror had a built-in television, and the flooring was made up of heated tiles. It was a futuristic lap of luxury.

Because of our height, we could view Baku all the way to the Caspian Sea on one side of the room. On the other side, we could see the slums below us, hidden behind the walls we had passed by on our ride into town. Quickly we realized that, like so many places in our own country, there was a great divide between the rich and poor, with the concentration of the rich in a small area and the poor hidden away.

After our tour, we finally had a chance to take Journey out so he could use the bathroom. He traveled all the way back down the elevator and never complained once. He was such a good sport about it. He truly had a bladder and butt of steel.

WHERE IN THE WORLD IS AZERBAIJAN?

What is it about sitting on a plane for twenty-two hours that makes you so tired?

I tend to be light sensitive when I sleep, and the Flame Towers lit up the night sky, making it difficult, initially, for me to go to bed. Luckily, when I lowered the shades, the room was pitch black. It worked wonderfully, and I slept until seven the next morning, at which point I excitedly raised the blinds to admire the view with fresh eyes. My parents blinked sleepily and yelled at me to stop waking them up "in the middle of the night"! I guess they needed more time to adjust to the time difference than I did. Me? I was ready to see what adventures the day would bring.

We were scheduled to be in Azerbaijan for a week. The first few days were dedicated to sightseeing with a personal tour guide assigned to our group. It became clear fairly quickly that it wasn't a country where it was advisable to speak your opinions. At one point on the tour, our guide said something that was almost-but-not-quite-negative about the people in power. I don't believe it was intentional; it seemed to be a slip of the tongue. But our guide quickly backtracked when the woman accompanying him on the tour bus corrected his language. After that we were told, "This government is awesome. They've made our people taller."

I saw no others with visible disabilities on the street during my stay. Handicap access was not available anywhere. As I rolled around with my service dog, people would turn and stare openly, and some seemed to think I had a cognitive disability and treated me accordingly. I had to assume that because they didn't regularly see people with disabilities, they simply weren't familiar with it. I have often wondered if it's because those with disabilities are institutionalized and hidden away in that country; I have no way of knowing for sure. Still, it was isolating. My parents warned me not to go off on my own and act like I was in America because they were worried about how I might be received.

In fact, my whole family was told not to go off the beaten path. But my parents wanted to experience the *real* Azerbaijan. My father wanted to visit an art museum, and so he pulled up GPS directions on his phone, and because we are a family of adventurers, off we set.

We got lost. Of course we did! And where did we end up? Off the beaten path that we were warned against leaving!

My dad was pushing me in my wheelchair, rolling me through a not-so-nice part of the city. There were giant curbs everywhere, and I had to be wheeled up and over, then down and over, constantly. There were stray cats everywhere that Journey seemed to want to befriend. My parents told me, "Don't you dare let him meet one of these cats!" I didn't, but I thought it would have been cute.

As we rolled awkwardly on our way, we had the opportunity to meet locals who were amazingly friendly. One vendor was selling traditional silk scarves, which were beautiful, and everyone we met was inviting

 BEYOND EXPECTATIONS

and proud to show off their wares and their culture. I may have been in the country to receive an award, but the most amazing experience was to get lost, lift the curtain, and learn about Azerbaijan from the local people, who clearly loved sharing their world with a family of enthusiastic tourists.

Finally, the night we were waiting for came about. I was able to get dressed up in my gorgeous evening gown, and off we went to the celebration hall. It was packed to the brim. Journey was my "plus one"! Because of the sheer number of people, the room was loud, and for much of the night Journey stayed underneath our table, hidden away to protect his sensitive ears.

During the reception, traditional music played, with heavy drums and dancers. Holograms of horses appeared to race around the room. The effect was mind-blowing, and that was just the introduction to the evening!

Soon, Journey and I were whisked away to prepare to roll on stage and accept my award. Backstage, I felt so cool as I met Princess Haya bint Al Hussein of Jordan, an equestrian and President of the FEI from 2006 to 2014. Fun fact: She was the second princess Journey got to meet and impress, earning a pat for his good manners. And then we were met with the most amazing surprise: Journey received a trophy of his own in the form of a dog bowl!

The awards presentation was only the beginning of the evening. It was followed by a traditional feast. (There was cumin in almost everything!) When our waiter brought our food, Journey was once again under the table, hiding from the noise. The server noticed him, pointed, and asked in English, "Sheep?"

"No, no, no—a dog!" I reassured him. I didn't want to laugh, but I thought it was completely hilarious. If Journey had understood our brief exchange, I knew he would have been mortally offended.

The server asked to pet Journey, explaining, "Here, we usually have

German Shepherds or protection dogs."

But who brings a sheep to a gala?

◇ ◇ ◇

Anyone who knows me knows that if there is a dance floor, I will be on it. I am a *shameless* dancer. When there is music, I'm moving and grooving.

After dinner, I noticed a man and woman dancing in the center of a circle people had made for them. I wanted to dance in the circle too and be the center of attention. I rolled over, bopping away, and made my entrance. I strutted my thing in my wheelchair, feeling myself. When the song was over, I rolled out of the circle back toward our table, and the FEI liaison came up to me and asked, "Sydney, you know who you just danced with, don't you?"

"No, why?" I admit I was curious, but really, I was just dancing like I always do. It wasn't like I was trying to marry him or anything.

"That was the President of Azerbaijan."

Who else but me would drop in on a dance circle for a foreign leader? I realized then that the circle was probably out of respect and not indicative of the dance battle I assumed it was.

Still, I regretted nothing. Obviously, he wanted to dance with me!

The event was fantastic.

Besides becoming a president's surprise dream woman, I had the opportunity to meet the winner of another award—the Rising Star recipient, Lambert LeClézio, a vaulter from Mauritius, an island nation in the Indian Ocean. We were the same age, and our parents clicked, so we spent a lot of time together. We formed a friendship, and it made me so happy to share such an incredible experience with a friend.

Winning the Against All Odds Award, and being recognized in such a way, rekindled my fire to win medals and keep pushing through my challenges to achieve my goals. I saw the hard work paying off, but I also realized that others around the world were watching me and cheering me on. What I was doing became more and more about being a role model than winning a competition.

◇ ◇ ◇

Our flight left Azerbaijan super early in the morning. My parents assured me they would handle the packing details, then wake me up, right when it was time to go. They decided to take Journey out at about one in the morning, but hey, the dog must go before a twenty-two-hour flight. It had to be done.

As they exited the hotel, they turned right, forgetting we had been told we should never walk in that direction. Before they realized their mistake, they heard someone yell, "Stop!"

And the sound of multiple guns' safeties turning off.

My dad moved and stepped in front of my mom, as it became clear on the darkened street that armed guards had machine guns aimed at them. The tension was incredibly high, so of course that was the moment Journey chose to take care of business.

Because...of course.

There was my mom, probably thinking, *"They're going to kill us, we'll leave our kid stranded in Azerbaijan"*—all of it probably firing through her brain while Journey was squatting on the ground, completely unaware of his audience or the imminent danger.

Luckily, my parents were allowed to turn around and return to the hotel, where the concierge was horrified to discover they had turned right and headed toward the heavily guarded Government House.

Never a dull moment. Of course, I was sleeping peacefully in my hotel room while all this went down. My parents woke me up with, "Sydney, you were almost an orphan!"

Because Azerbaijan was not used to service dogs, we added time to how far ahead we figured we needed to go to the airport and get through security. We knew that having Journey with us could cause complications. We set out with a lot of time to spare.

Out of concern for the safety of the other passengers, because I had Journey, the airline moved all the Business Class passengers to First Class and told us we'd have to stay in Business Class by ourselves.

How unfortunate for us!

Partway through the flight, the attendant asked us, "Is that all he does?" She looked at Journey as he lay sleeping on the floor in front of us—now a seasoned traveler. One of the mothers who had been moved to First Class had small children and commented on how she wished her own children would be as well mannered. Journey always showed others how a gentleman behaved and left a good impression of service dogs in their minds.

Upon arrival back in the United States, my father continued on to Michigan and my little brothers, and Mom and I went upstate where I started training again and life resumed for the two weeks leading up to Christmas.

Usually, my family celebrated the holidays by the seat of our pants, but that year was special. On December twenty-second, my grandparents, dad, and brothers drove from Michigan to Millbrook, where we were going to celebrate. On Christmas Eve, we all piled into a couple cars and headed to the mall to "start" our shopping. My brothers and I ran full tilt around the shops to secure the best gifts we could at the last minute. Sweaty and laughing, we met back up in the evening, only to realize, "Crap, we forgot a tree!" So at six o'clock on Christmas Eve, in Danbury, Connecticut, we pulled into a lot where we could see two gigantic, beautiful trees. The manager said they were already taken and waiting to be picked up. My grandparents, siblings, and I waited in the car while my parents went off on their own to try and solve the problem. They came back, grinning broadly, proudly holding up a bough that had fallen off or been cut off another tree, calling out, "We got a free tree!" I still can't think about it without laughing hysterically.

Back home, I decorated the scanty tree limb, which somehow still fit into the tree stand (I'm surprised the screw went that far in) with a handful of ornaments. It was our very own Charlie Brown Christmas Tree. Somehow, no matter how it came together, the holidays were always special.

NORTH AMERICANS

In 2015, for the first time, para dressage was added to the North American Junior Young Rider Championships in Kentucky. It was four years after my demo at the Kentucky Horse Park, which Jonathan had been instrumental in making happen.

After my experience with WEG and the two unbelievable award recognitions, finding that a goal Jonathan and I had set forth to achieve together was coming to fruition was so heartwarmingly astonishing to me. Have you ever felt like sometimes things just line up the way they were meant? So often, we focus on "bad things happening in threes." Alternatively, good things can happen in clusters, also. Looking back, I can see how everything changed for the better in just a few, short years, opening opportunities that hadn't been possible when I first entered the sport.

I knew I could do it.

After returning from Azerbaijan and into the spring, Wes and I focused on rehabilitating Wentworth. It was a long, slow road in the cold northeastern winter, but our focus was building him up to be stronger than ever before. Wentworth was, by nature, a relatively laid-back Hanoverian. However, after six months of strict stall rest, he had become a fire-breathing dragon. It was interesting to have an angsty, hot horse that my trainer needed to school and ride before I could work with him safely.

Once he was determined to be strong and sound, Wentworth became my go-to competition horse—something we'd always intended for him. We showed at HITS Saugerties, Schenectady, and Stockade, and a few more international competitions where he found himself back in the rhythm again. His natural laziness reemerged with the regular workload. I got into a bad habit where my right leg would be overactive to counterbalance my left side, while also constantly encouraging him forward as best I could. Still, as slow as he was, Wentworth gave me his all.

At the North American Championships, I remember walking Wentworth while put-putting around in my scooter, trying to make it through the mud. The grass itself, however, was pristine and gorgeous—everything you expect Kentucky to look like.

A friend of mine from Michigan was stabled one barn aisle down. I knew Maxine from my earliest riding days and my original eventing barn, and I was so impressed she was now a trainer with a student competing at North Americans.

Many of the kids I'd ridden with didn't make it as eventers. Cedar Ridge, our barn, weeded out the weak. The owner of the barn got her horses from a rescue organization, and they had little training or experience. Not a rider herself, the owner trained young kids to train other young kids on semi-feral horses.

I was accustomed to a way of training that involved yelling and pointing out your flaws. As a positive person, this type of training never really got me down, and it prepared me for working with Wes later in my life, as this was his style of "teaching" as well. Some people prefer warm and fuzzy. Me, I just needed someone who would turn me into a better rider, to help me become more critical of myself, and pick apart my rides in order to help me always strive for perfection.

There were about six super-senior horses at that first barn who were saints. Then there were some legitimately weird horses! Despite the questionable strategies for training young riders, I have great memories of the horses at Cedar Ridge and the experience I gained there at an early age. So, seeing Maxine again, so many years later, was such a serendipitous moment—it was only one of the few times over the years we crossed paths at random.

During that first year back in the saddle, competing on my own horse, I felt like Jonathan was riding with me, silently watching as I worked toward a goal—one we'd both had for para dressage, *together*. I always rode with a favorite photo of the two of us in my pocket, so that he was literally riding right down centerline with me. I've felt driven by a larger force beyond my own ambition since his loss. In the scheme of things, we'd only known each other a short while, but he had an everlasting impact on my life.

When North Americans finally arrived in our first year that included para dressage, there were only a few juniors or young riders. There were only three competitors from the United States, with me once again the youngest of the group, competing against a three-rider team for Canada.

Any time I rode into the show ring it was a great day.

At North Americans, we had an opportunity to compete with and against able-bodied riders for the same FEI medals, which was a unique situation. Wentworth and I medaled and won the gold. The true highlight of the show, however, was finally having the ability to ride my own horse in competition, something bad luck—or whatever you want to call it—had prevented until that moment.

I was incredibly impressed with my teammate, Cambry Kaylor. She had been paralyzed from the waist down in an equestrian vaulting accident, but the loss of the use of her legs did not keep her from the back of a horse—she was back in the saddle only months after her injuries, and eventually discovered she could still actually *ride.*

At the beginning of one of her tests at the North American Championships, Cambry's horse bucked, and her safety straps came undone. She had to complete the test without being held on the horse. I watched her and thought, *Wow, that's a teammate.* If Cambry had forfeited, our entire team would have been out of the medals because we didn't have a drop score. She was willing to finish her test however she could to support the team who relied on her. That is the sort of teammate that I've always hoped to be, putting the team first. We had to have each other's backs.

Even though Jonathan wasn't there in person, his happiness, team spirit, and camaraderie carried over, even three years after his passing. His legacy remained vibrant and alive.

2015 was the first and only year para dressage was represented at the North Americans to date. I would love to see Canada and the United States foster youth talent who aspire to compete at the higher levels in the sport. There is a lot of work that still needs to be done to mentor and foster opportunities for para riders to be set up for success so they can be better prepared to compete on international soil in a team setting at events like the World Equestrian Games and the Paralympics.

Our youth is the future of our sport. The United States has now hired a Development Coach to work with riders and mentor them across state lines, including states like Michigan that might be more set apart from the nexus of competition in Wellington, Florida. Not everyone has the money, time, or opportunity to move across the country for a trainer and upend their entire lives in pursuit of their competitive goals. Accessibility is probably the biggest barrier for my sport.

In the United States, the geographic expanse of the country serves as a unique challenge, and many riding facilities are in rural areas and trainers have to travel great distances with riders and horses to compete in qualifying events. Europe, by comparison, has a large number of Concourse Para Equestre de Dressage International (CPEDI) competitions in a relatively small area, so many American riders find it easier to travel internationally over the spring and summer and hit several shows in a short amount of time overseas.

Although the qualifying race was real and I aimed to ride at the Paralympics, I was more and more focused on becoming a mentor to developing riders. I wanted to live by example, yes, but also be someone they could come to with questions, advice, and more. Anyone can ask me anything at any time. I'm always a friend to a young rider. I know that the sport can be overwhelming when you are first starting out. It had taken a lot of sacrifice to move from Michigan, but the one thing I never had to do without was the support of mentors and family.

And I want that for every aspiring rider.

QUALIFICATION YEAR

21

Time flew in a whirlwind of competitions and awards ceremonies. Suddenly it was 2015, and it was the qualification year for the 2016 Summer Paralympics in Rio de Janeiro.

I had Wentworth back in full training and had also been given the opportunity to free-lease a horse named Scampano ("Scampi") from his owner, who was based at a barn in New Jersey. In addition, my trainer generously gave me the opportunity to partner with a mare named Rosie who had been to the 2012 Paralympics with rider Donna Ponessa and was an established high-level competition horse. Once again, I found myself in training with multiple horses, which continued to challenge me as a rider as I adapted to each of their riding styles.

Rosie was the sort of mare who always had her guard up. She also needed a lot of strength and communication in the reins, which was a learning curve for me with my particular disability. She was very forward-thinking, compared to Wentworth, who sometimes had to be nagged to move! A horse that generated her own forward momentum was not only a big advantage because a forward tendency can be rewarded by judges in dressage, but because of my own physical limitations. Since I had to continually nag Wentworth with my leg to get him to move forward, it became a challenge for my body to keep him straight and balanced. Rosie, on the other hand, was already "forward," so I could focus on my body more correctly and just let her carry me. Her spicy and opinionated personality reminded me of one of my earliest horses, Lacey, and similarly, Rosie challenged me a lot. No ride was spot on or magical. She swiftly became bored in the arena, so we spent a lot of time walking outside the fence or on road rides so she wouldn't become sour.

I never focused on the challenging parts of my horse partnerships. A rough training ride might be having to do a 10-meter circle at the trot until I got it right, regardless of how many times it took. Wes was a taskmaster and repetition was his method. Compliments were incredibly rare; they were cherished when they were received. As I've mentioned, I was never treated like I had a disability—the bar set for me was the same as an able-bodied rider, if not held higher. I felt I was lucky to find a trainer who treated me like the rest of his clients, and even tougher at times. I never settled for less because of my disability.

It would have been easy to focus on the harder rides or get angry and frustrated. Instead, I made the conscious decision to focus on the best parts of each lesson: "My circle felt much rounder in this direction today," or "My arm felt more stable, and I needed less correction today." The "silver linings" were always there, even on my toughest days. I always had a nagging voice telling me what I could have done better, but I never let the intrusive thoughts get to me. Instead, I aimed to use them as constructive criticism to help me improve my next ride.

My mom often questioned if Rosie was the right fit for me, but I had faith in this horse and her talent. She never made my rides easy, but I learned a lot from her and the challenges she presented me with during our time together. After my years catch riding different horses at every show, having six months with one mare seemed like a lifetime.

Scampano, on the other hand, was a beautiful, talented 17.2-hand dark bay gelding with a trot that went on for days and an adjustable mind and level head. My biggest challenge with him was that he did not have the best walk. When fifty percent of your test at a competition is at the walk—well, you can probably guess how that went. Nonetheless, he was a joy to ride and taught me a lot in his own way, as all horses do (and his owner was always amazed that I stayed on and was able to manage a trot as big as his!).

Wentworth, Scampano, and Rosie came to Florida with us for the winter show and training season. Wes determined Wellington was too expensive that year, so we found a barn in Lake City, Florida, which is north of Gainesville. We knew nothing about the area but assumed everywhere in Florida would be hot. We learned the hard way that each region of Florida has its own climate. Sadly, we had only packed shorts and summer-appropriate gear when leaving New York. It was a very unhappy surprise to find that parts of Florida did, in fact, have a kind of "winter," and we'd be in the depths of it.

We stayed at a barn that had been part of a top-of-the-line equestrian center that had never taken off or become the popular eventing barn it was built to be. Rather than competing with crowds and sharing stabling with a bunch of strangers, we had the entire facility to ourselves, with only nine horses in total.

While some might lament spending the winter season in a sort of "ghost town," I enjoyed the opportunity to have fewer distractions and just focus on my rides as I trained with all three horses. There were large open fields where we could hack, allowing for the kind of cross-training that helps keep performance horses mentally and physically at their peak by avoiding drilling test after test into their brains.

Moreover, the series of unplanned events our location in Florida brought us meant that we had to learn to adjust to situations. I am very driven, but that could sometimes make it hard for me to go with the flow and learn how to make something work for me, even if I didn't anticipate the manner which it occurred.

Both Wentworth and Rosie did well at competitions that season and were meeting scores neck and neck. Scampi's were less than optimal because of the poor quality of his walk, so it didn't make sense to compete him, despite how much I loved riding him. Wentworth and Rosie's evenness was surprising in many ways, considering how different they were in their personalities and movement. I would ride Rosie (if, at a show, her time was first), do our test, then dismount and work on completely changing my approach. Two different horses and two different rides, back-to-back. It was a high-pressure environment, but I had to learn to ride the horse I had underneath me. I had no choice.

I actually thrived in that situation, because I couldn't overthink it. I had a history of writing down cues, drawing out the geometry of the test and the arena, and being too much in my head. That just didn't work with this scenario.

◇ ◇ ◇

I'm an extrovert. I love people, and those who have met me in person know that I can talk anyone's ear off. I love to be surrounded with family and friends. By sixteen, I had already learned some harsh lessons about how not all friendships are meant to last. It still hurt that, back when I was first diagnosed with Wyburn-Mason syndrome, my best friend and I had drifted apart. I'm sure that seeing your friend facing brain damage and loss of mobility is scary, but it hurt me to lose her, because I lived in fear and needed peers, especially someone who I'd spent nearly every day with growing up. I figured out how to move on, as painful as it was, and eventually found friends at the barn or through my support groups.

Moving from Michigan to New York, focusing on my goals to compete, doing a lot of my studies online—all of this meant that finding and keeping close friends could be hard. My true friendships, though, shined through over the years.

One of my best barn friends from back in New York, Satu, came to Florida and groomed for me at the CPEDIs (the FEI-level competitions), and rode and trained on her own leased horse while we were in Lake City. Having a friend to talk to, and who believed in me, made a huge difference in my general outlook. It was incredible that she was willing and able to come to Florida for the winter, and I cherished our time together, whether it was at horse shows or hanging out on our couch at our shared apartment after rides. She put her all into helping me do my very best and into making my horses shine their brightest when it really counted, and that is something I will forever be grateful to her for!

SELECTION TRIALS

graduated high school in the summer of 2015 and took a gap year to focus on competing and making the US Para Dressage Team. The time away from the pressure of studying allowed me to find myself without "school" looming in the back of my mind. After the Paralympics in Rio de Janeiro, I would think about what I wanted to do academically. But until then, I wanted to have all eyes on the prize.

The Selection Trials in early June were amazing. Both Rosie and Wentworth were great, and the greatest benefit was that the Trials took place in Michigan, on my home turf. I felt incredibly confident surrounded by my family who were there to cheer me on. It felt like I'd been working my whole life to reach that point. Every challenge, every difficult moment had been merely a blip in time as my focus narrowed and I zeroed in on my goal to compete in the Paralympics for the first time. Despite my young age (I was only eighteen at the time), I'd already been through things many able-bodied athletes would never experience. I had lived a full life, and it all had been with the goal of reaching this moment.

Friends who still lived in Michigan—from high school and my old barn—came to watch me compete. It felt like coming home. It had been years since I'd seen many of them, and knowing they were in the crowd, supporting me after all the time that had passed, felt like my biggest achievement.

I won the National Championships on Rosie that year, right in my own backyard. Rosie competed her heart out while still challenging me every day of the show with her "mare-ish" ways. I never knew which side of her personality I would get, and working with her made me resilient. She made me feel like I could do anything.

After the show, I was called into a "super-secret meeting" onsite, and that was where I was informed that I had made the Paralympic Team! But…I couldn't announce it publicly. The United States Equestrian Foundation, which governed the sport, had to make the announcement first. There was an embargo on sharing the news for *two full weeks*. Waiting had never been so difficult! I wanted to shout the results from the rooftops and tell everyone on the street who walked past! NO ONE could know—not my family, not my trainer, NO ONE. I would have to privately count down the days until I could go public and acknowledge what was a huge accomplishment for me.

Before we left the showgrounds at the Selection Trials, those named to the team and as alternates had to take a drug test right away. As you may remember, the whole "pee in the cup" requirement was a particular challenge for me. The interesting thing was the grounds in Michigan did not have handicap-accessible bathrooms.

Oh, boy.

The test officials had a script they read to us and a very strict protocol to follow. I found it fascinating, and it made me feel pretty important. The trouble was, I had to complete the test independently. With no handicap accessible restroom and a single working hand, let's just

 BEYOND EXPECTATIONS

33. One of the few photos I have with my friend and mentor Jonathan Wentz. We were always having a great time together!

34. Wth my first service dog Journey. His snuggles were the best.

35 & 36. With Wentworth, my first real para horse, it was love at first kiss, to say the least.

Above photo by Susan J. Stickle

37. On Willi Wesley, owned by Victoria Dugan, at the 2014 World Equestrian Games in Normandy, France.
Photo by Susan J. Stickle

38. Journey proudly sporting his World Equestrian Games accredidations. He was the real superstar!

Photo by Luc Percival

39. Willi Wesley strutting his stuff in the competition arena at WEG 2014.

Photo by Susan J. Stickle

 Receiving the Junior Equestrian of the Year
honor at the USEF Pegasus Awards in 2014, with
Journey right by my side as he deserved, and sharing
the stage with Judy Werner (Lifetime Achievement
Award) and my idol Olympian Beezie Madden (her
fourth Equestrian of the Year trophy).

41. Receiving the FEI Against All Odds Award. Leave it to Journey to take the award as an opportunity to sneak a kiss from Princess Haya, then president of the FEI. *Photo by FEI / Liz Gregg*

Odds
Sydney

42 & 43. Michelle Obama spoke at the "100 Days to Rio" live recording in Times Square...and then gave me a hug! A true high point of my life!

44. Paralympic Training Camp in Florida was full of so many great rides and so many smiles! Besides me, our Rio Team included (above, left to right): Rebecca Hart ("Becca"), Margaret McIntosh ("Gigi"), and Annie Peavy, with Roxanne Trunnell ("Roxie") riding as an individual.

45. Landing in Brazil, the anticipation was real!

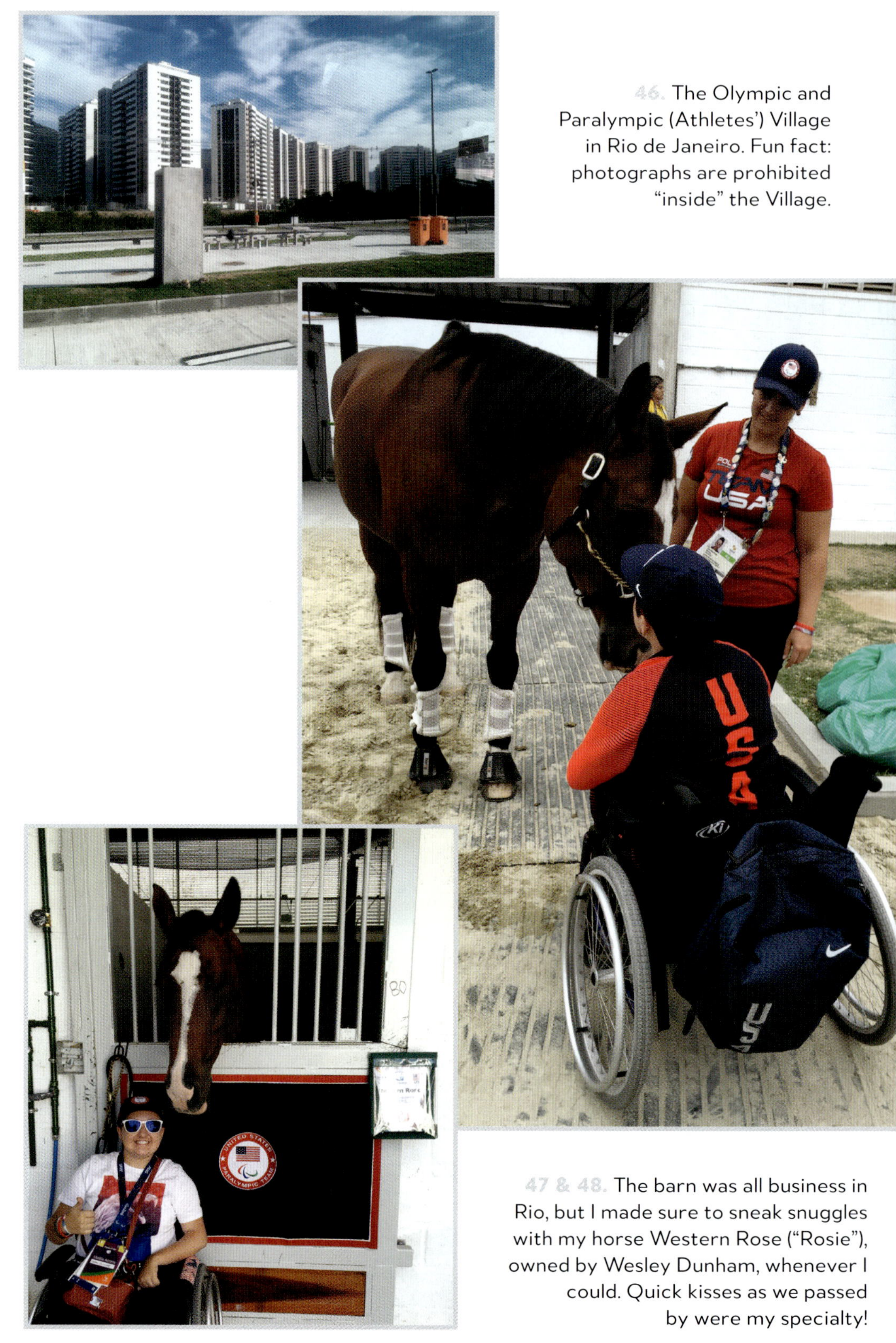

46. The Olympic and Paralympic (Athletes') Village in Rio de Janeiro. Fun fact: photographs are prohibited "inside" the Village.

47 & 48. The barn was all business in Rio, but I made sure to sneak snuggles with my horse Western Rose ("Rosie"), owned by Wesley Dunham, whenever I could. Quick kisses as we passed by were my specialty!

49 & 50. Warmup days in Rio went off without a hitch thanks to my awesome groom Amy and trainer Wes. We were in great shape heading into the competition arena.

Inset photo by John Stroud

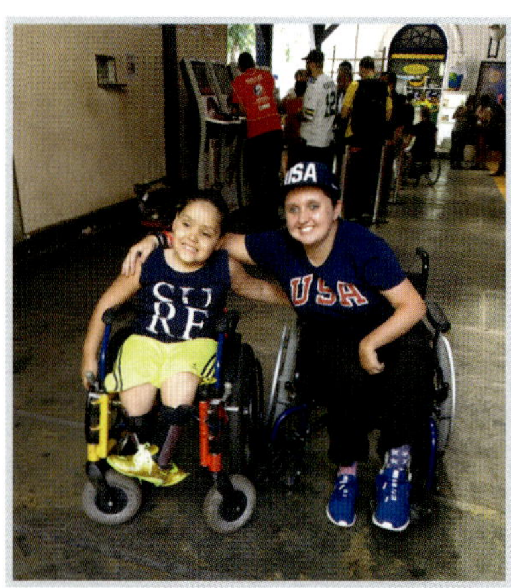

51. I couldn't have asked for a better group of friends and athletes to share the experience of my first Paralympic Games.

52 & 53. A chance meeting with a young Brazilian on our way to Christ the Redeemer in Rio de Janeiro made a big impact on me. Being a role model for others has always been my goal. Then holding the torch with my teammates at the top sealed a successful Paralympic debut. Hope was in the air.

54. Rosie sporting her well-deserved seventh-place ribbon from the Individual Test!

55 & 56. What a thrill it was to be part of Team USA's visit to The White House! My hair was President Obama-approved.

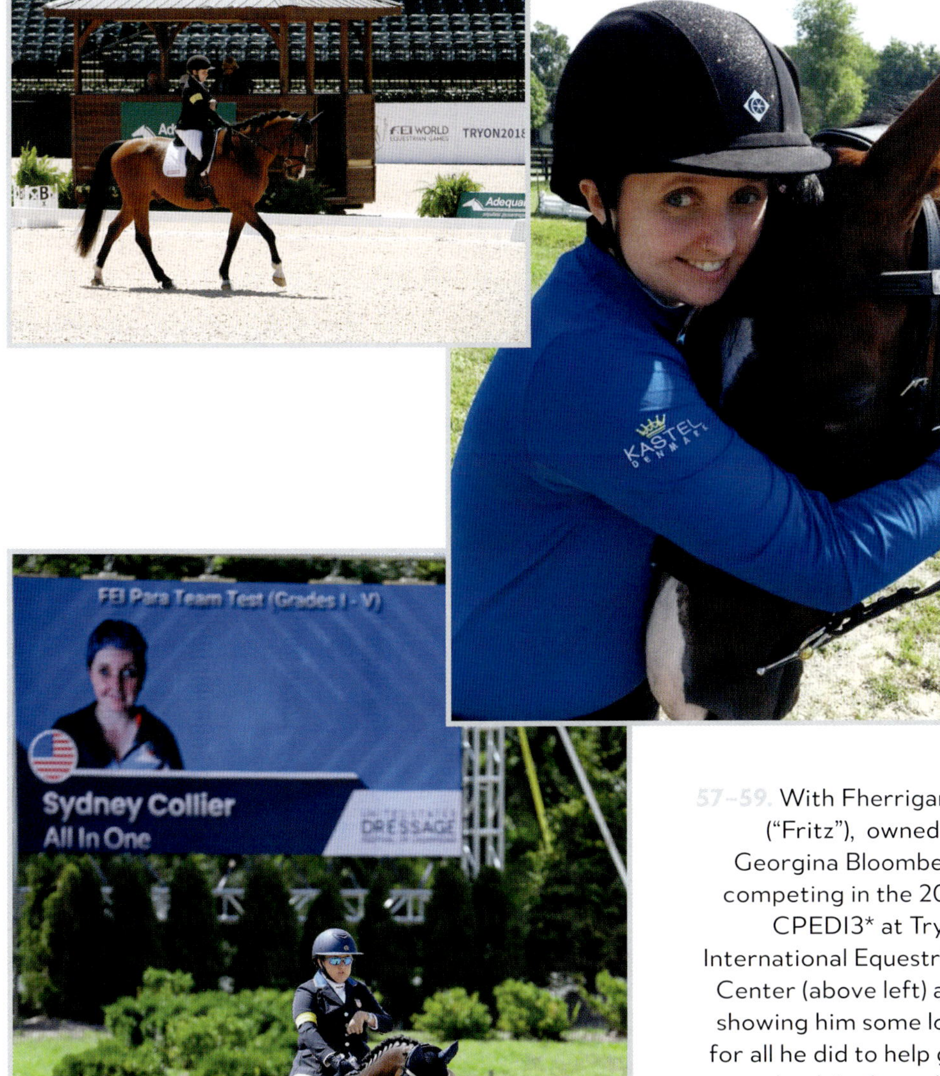

57–59. With Fherrigamo ("Fritz"), owned by Georgina Bloomberg, competing in the 2018 CPEDI3* at Tryon International Equestrian Center (above left) and showing him some love for all he did to help get me get back in the saddle after my fifth stroke (above). And on All in One ("Alle"), a gelding owned by Georgina who I began competing in 2019 (left).

Above left photo by Lara Ceppi; left photo by Susan J. Stickle

60. I can't wait to see what happens next!

Photo by Susan J. Stickle

say that, once again, the procuring a sample was a challenge in and of itself. The official stood outside an open door while I tried, rather clumsily, to make the required deposit.

I passed with flying colors, if a little awkwardly. Looking back, it always gives me a giggle when I think about how, historically, the pee tests were more difficult for me than the riding part of the competitions!

I was then given an app on my phone to continue drug testing protocol. Olympic and Paralympic athletes have to log our locations at all times so a testing official can randomly show up at any time. I took it very seriously, because if an official showed up and you were twenty minutes late, you could be banned from competing. I didn't want to let myself or my team down, so it became almost a compulsive need for me to log my location every few minutes.

After the Selection Trials, I kept my same training schedule until one month prior to the Paralympics. It's important to note that even at the highest level of competition, most athletes, horse and rider both, don't give 100 percent each time we train. We build a lot of foundation, we change up our routines, and we make sure to go on hacks and have lazy days where we can clear our heads and just enjoy the ride. All of this avoids burnout in both our bodies and our minds, helping to avoid injury and keeping us focused mentally.

Rosie was also a horse that couldn't and wouldn't be pushed hard for a long time. We needed to ramp up our training slowly so she would peak once we were in Brazil.

The best way to explain how I train is that each day I work on individual pieces of the puzzle—fine-tuning them and varying them— so that during a competition I am prepared to put them all together and complete the image. It's easy in dressage to fall into a pattern of drilling a test over and over, so the test itself was something I would only work on once or twice a week at most. Instead, I would focus on my free walk one day, a ten-meter circle the next, and so on. Making the individual parts of our performance shine resulted in a beautiful softness and prevented us from pushing too hard. When I sensed that Rosie seemed a little bored with the arena, I would spend time walking around the outside of the ring, letting her do something more interesting to her. Considering what horses need is an incredibly important part of working with them. They are not machines and shouldn't be treated as such.

As two athletes in a partnership, the mental aspect of the sport is just as important as the physical. Communication is key between horse and rider. Rosie had such a personality that she demanded I listen to her, and it made for a wonderful challenge because I frequently had to pivot and focus on what she needed from me on a particular day. There is a clear difference between a horse that is happy with his job and a horse that is "shut down." This is especially important when riding at the Olympic level, where points that can determine medals come down to the finest movements and slightest suspension of the body. A horse that is dull and bored, having drilled the exercises, will never be a winner. The same can be said for the rider. Overthinking and overdrilling can lead to boredom and the rider missing important small communications from the horse.

One of the biggest things that has made me a better rider has been working with a sport psychologist who gave me tools to become a better "mental athlete." I feel the difference when I compete, and I also know, without a doubt, the mental aspect is hugely important for my partner—my horse. If my mind is clear and focused, we can better tune in to each other. This is something I wish I had known in the lead up to my first Paralympic Games, but I was not yet aware of the importance of "strengthening the mental muscle."

Training as an equestrian becomes more about working smart and not necessarily hard. I was fortunate to have a trainer who understood that in the lead up to Rio. Additionally, I was able to continue riding Wentworth, so I rode twice a day, six days a week, as well as doing Pilates and general workouts at a gym nearby in Millbrook.

◇ ◇ ◇

In July, my mom received an invitation to the "100 Days to Rio" recording of the *Today Show* in New York City. We jumped at the opportunity and replied at once.

I love the city; there is no place like it. The crowd energy is electric for an extrovert like me. When I am there, I talk to everyone I can, and those who live there probably think I am ridiculous. While I was training upstate, we went in often, and I always had a great time.

Team USA paid for my mom and Journey and I to stay at the Hilton near Times Square. When we arrived, I picked up my official Paralympic uniform and met with show staff to discuss what we should expect during the live recording the next day.

A select group of Olympians and Paralympians had been asked to be part of the show, and I was so honored to be included in their ranks. It was the first time I got to meet other athletes from different sports, like Tatyana McFadden, who was a Paralympic track gold medalist, and an idol of mine. It was incredible to meet her in person. I was happy to have Journey by my side, who opened a lot of conversations.

The morning of the big day we met in the hotel conference room. The production assistants informed us, "Okay, this is going to be very exciting. We have a guest speaker today who you will be meeting and a musical act, The Band Perry."

I didn't know the band, as I was not into country music, but I was excited to hear their performance anyway—and get autographs!

We weren't told who the speaker would be but had to fill out an intense amount of paperwork. I and the other athletes were trying to guess who it could be when in walked the First Lady at the time, Michelle Obama.

I lost my mind.

So, I guess the Secret Service knows everything about me now.

As all the different news outlets filed in to interview Michelle Obama and the athletes in a pre-show media blitz, I realized that for para dressage to be represented on this international stage was a life-changing opportunity. I had always wanted to stand for and grow my sport through raising awareness about it, and this was my chance.

While Michelle Obama gave a speech for the *Today Show*, the athletes all stood behind her on stage. (Well, all the athletes except for Journey, because he didn't have the necessary security clearance. Because he didn't put paw to paper, he had to remain with my mom off stage.) The speech was incredibly moving, and she turned to shake everyone's hands afterward. Then the person just before me went in for a hug. We were allowed to do that? Obviously, I was not missing such an opportunity. It was Michelle Obama, and we were on live TV—I had to go for it! After I gave her a hug, I spoke with her for a few moments. What a feeling!

After my unbelievable interaction with Michelle Obama, Hoda Kotb, the *Today Show* co-host, came over and said hello to all of us while The Band Perry was playing. What a surreal experience. I was eighteen years old and surrounded by incredible energy and amazing athletes and world leaders. There are no words I can use to truly express how it felt at the time to be among them and giving my all to the movement that my mentor Jonathan had started. Like him, I wanted to make changes in the world, and I wanted to see them happen before me. My goal continued to develop into something more than winning medals. I had always hoped to be an advocate and empower others to see their potential and feel like their own goals were achievable. Now it felt like the universe was helping me achieve this by giving me a platform. I knew anything was truly possible.

BOOTCAMP

Running up to Rio, I entered a few national shows in the Northeast with both Rosie and Wentworth and earned some of our best scores to date. I felt ready and excited for what was to come.

Paralympic Training Camp took place in Ocala, Florida. We spent a week and a half as a team, while our horses quarantined together. The Team consisted of myself, Annie Peavy, Margaret McIntosh ("Gigi"), and Rebecca Hart ("Becca"), with Roxanne Trunnell ("Roxie") riding as an individual. While all of us lived and competed in different regions of the United States, we were good friends and knew each other well already because our sport was so small, which helped solidify us as a team more quickly. The venue was nice, we were all together for the first time, and it set a good tone for the next few weeks as we bonded together more closely. We went from competitors to teammates, and Camp was a great way to build relationships with the other riders.

The Team had two personal care assistants, and we all stayed in a house on the barn property. Gigi and Becca stayed together, Roxy and Annie shared a room, and I was the odd one out.

Journey had stayed at home with my Uncle Bob. We were unsure whether the Brazilian authorities would let him return to the United States if he traveled with me to Rio de Janeiro. We couldn't get a firm answer whether quarantine would be two days or six months, and we were unwilling to risk him having to stay behind without one of us. We all felt that my making the trip without him was the safer decision. And I wasn't worried about him getting a little vacation!

Some members of the Team's parents came to Training Camp to lend support as needed so things would go smoothly. Our trainers and grooms were also in attendance. Amy, Wentworth's former owner, came once again to groom for me, as she had at WEG. I guess her previous experience had been a positive one!

We went light on practice with the horses at Training Camp. Our goal was to make sure the horses were fit and had plenty of "gas in the tank" for international travel and competition.

I was able to be a bit more independent while at Camp, and as a result, my mom spent a lot of time with Annie's mom, Becky. This was a great test for us since parents do not enter the Athlete's Village at the Paralympics, so I would truly be on my own for the first time in my life in Brazil. It was a big change for both my mom and for me, and it made me miss her. We'd been a team for so long that it was a bit of an adjustment to go through my day to day without her, but it was nice having a little autonomy.

After the Training Camp quarantine period, the Team horses flew on a FedEx cargo plane out of Miami directly to Brazil. My groom Amy was selected to travel with the horses ahead of the rest of us. They were on their way!

It was finally time for "Team Processing." The entire United States Paralympic team traveled to Houston, Texas, for two days where we would prepare for our time in Rio as representatives of our country. All Paralympians descended on a hotel for media training, rule training, and lots of information. At the hotel, I roomed with Annie. She was nineteen, and this was the first Paralympic Games for us both. I loved having a roommate, especially one around my own age.

Two weeks prior to our media training, the now-infamous incident with swimmer Ryan Lochte (fabricating a story about a robbery to cover up some alcohol-related behavior) had occurred in Rio de Janeiro. The Paralympics traditionally are held directly after the Olympics, and because of the "Lochtegate" scandal, officials were extra thorough with our preparation, explaining repeatedly how we could be a "good" part of Team USA and honor our country as representatives.

Team USA representatives played an inspirational video and music, and passed out paper and envelopes so we could all write letters to ourselves addressing "The Post-Games You." I lost it and started sobbing. It felt like everything was *truly happening*. Writing a letter to my "post-games" self was mind-blowing. I knew everything was about to change in my life.

We also got our gear for the Games. We had standard, pre-approved, branded attire provided for our entire stay in Brazil. The only thing we could bring was our underwear and competition clothes.

Honestly, the swag was my favorite part! It was insane. The Nike gear shop was set up like a mall, but it was all free. Each athlete walked into a fitting room where a mirror glittered with your name in lights. Official attire in your size was picked out and brought to you VIP-style.

I wish I'd been told *not* to try on everything! Athletes were only supposed to try on one pair of pants, one shirt, one tank top, and a pair of shoes so sizing could be verified. I spent way too much time trying on clothes, which meant that I was then limited in my packing time. (I am someone who likes to organize and plan, and packing for a trip sometimes takes me two weeks ahead of a date of travel.) A team official actually had to come interrupt me in the dressing room and move me along! It was so embarrassing, but I'm glad they did it, because otherwise I would have been scrambling for time back in my room. Apparently, I tried on *everything*. What can I say? It was a learning experience!

Oakley provided four pairs of limited-edition sunglasses. In the same room, we each were given a limited-edition Omega watch! Ralph Lauren supplied our opening ceremony outfits. I felt like royalty. It was incredible. I ordered my Paralympic ring surrounded by the best athletes in the country, and we hadn't even competed yet.

It took me forever to get through the "free mall" setup in the hotel. I ended up in a hallway, alone, where I received two duffel bags full of gear. But everything we were going to take needed to be packed in a *single* bag. With the bag I'd packed and brought from home, I now had *three* bags that I needed to combine into one, somehow through magic, and without anyone's help. It seemed like everyone else was almost done repacking by the time I got started, so I felt very stressed, trying to merge everything in a short amount of time. I tend to be an "OCD packer"—highly organized and pre-planned. I don't just shove things into a bag. But here I was in a hallway with chaotic, disorganization all around me, trying to put everything together on my own in a short time with only one hand and one eye that could see. I was suddenly on the verge of a nervous breakdown. Here I was preparing for the most important competition of my life, and my bag was chaos, instilling a nervous energy that I hadn't had previously. I am such a planner and had everything I needed for the trip prepared, but now it seemed everything was thrown for a loop, and I had to reset mentally.

Luckily, my helmet, boots, and show gear had traveled with the horses, and so all of that was already in Rio de Janeiro, waiting for me, or I would have been a puddle of tears.

Somehow, I figured out what needed to travel with me and what could go, and my extra luggage and spare duffel were then packed to be returned to my home address. It was a real test of my newfound independence.

◇ ◇ ◇

We were in Houston only two days, then were picked up by shuttle buses to head to the airport, accompanied by a police escort.

I had my own entourage!

Our police escort gave us a "good luck" speech after dropping us, and local supporters came with signs, wishing Team USA success in Rio. We were on our way and wearing our team uniforms. This was the moment!

A dose of Benadryl ensured I got some rest on the plane. When I awoke, I'd be in Brazil and about to compete in my first Paralympics.

PARALYMPIC VILLAGE

While our flight to Brazil was commercial, there were not many passengers who weren't associated with the Paralympics. It was a plane full of athletes from the United States in their uniforms. It kicked off a series of events that allowed us to socialize and begin to function as one unit.

Of course, I slept through ninety-nine percent of the time in the air!

After landing in Brazil, we went through our first processing as a team. It took a few hours to complete checking in and to clear customs. Baggage claim was funny. We all had the same Nike duffle. Everyone's bag looked identical! The luggage tag was the only thing to discern yours from someone else's. It took an eternity to find which bag belonged to which owner.

Buses waited to take us from the airport to the Paralympic ("Athletes'")

Village. We were not allowed to travel individually or explore on our own. Everything was mass transit and chaperoned.

When I walked outside the airport, I was hit with a wall of tropical air. Summer in Texas, which we'd just left, was nothing to sneeze at, but the humidity in Brazil was another whole level of heat. In addition, all around the airport were armed guards. It was clear we were not in the United States anymore; it reminded me in some ways of my time in Azerbaijan.

Settled on the bus, I gazed upon the mountainous terrain, struck by the concentration of homes packed onto the sides of the hills, every color of the rainbow represented. The area was certainly more industrial than agricultural in feel. The sky seemed to be a whole new shade of blue that I hadn't ever experienced before—a luscious tropical sky that went on forever and represented the world of possibility that awaited me.

It took over an hour to reach our destination, and unloading took a long time as well, as we once again had to get our identical bags sorted. Checking in and out of the Village was like going through airport security. Guards scanned you, ran a wand over you, and checked your bags for contraband or dangerous weapons. Once screened through, I got my first view of the Paralympic Village.

It was surreal to consider how only two weeks before, the Olympics had been held in the same location, and multi-gold-medal-winning swimmer Michael Phelps had stayed there, walking through the same security checkpoint as me.

I had gone through Team USA training modules to prepare for our trip, but I really didn't know what to expect. *Wow.* The Village was its own civilization. It was made up of twenty to twenty-five high-rise buildings, each occupied by its own country, unless it was a smaller team. The construction was beautiful, despite having been done quickly. Unfortunately, it was clear the engineers had planned for the able-bodied athletes, and not the disabled. Not only were there limited elevators in our building, but those we had were incredibly slow. It was a bit of a problem with our wheelchairs and scooters.

We had sent our mobility scooters with the horses so that we could use them to get around in Brazil, but they were not capable of handling the Village in its entirety or our necessary trips to the barn. Halfway through the day, they would just die on us, and then we'd have to rely on someone pushing us around. We would take turns getting each other around, with one person riding a working scooter while propelling forward another person in their wheelchair while their scooter charged (partially, anyway) at home.

There were Village amenities, including a cafeteria with multiple stations, including Brazilian, American, Indian, and Asian. I was a very picky eater then, so my main meals during our stay were prepackaged chocolate muffins, pizza, and ice cream. The veggies and fruits had a peculiar chemical taste, due to official sanitization efforts, so I avoided them. These days I make better choices, knowing what I do about nutrition, but at that point, I saw food as more something to enjoy than as fuel and focused on the comfort food aspect. Looking back, I think the stress was more than I realized, and I was using food to calm myself.

I made some bad choices at the time, but I was an eighteen-year-old in a new country, and I simply focused on foods that were familiar to me. I've always had a complex relationship with food, something that I've worked on since, but it boiled over at the Games.

We also had a gym, nail salon, barber shop, and conveniently a wheelchair and mobility scooter repair store in the Village. McDonald's must have some sway because there was a storefront, and Samsung and a "Little Brazil market" were also there, and most everything was *free.*

I had no idea what to expect in terms of the living arrangements. Our Team was on one of the upper floors with an amazing view of the mountains from our balcony. It was a bright apartment with porcelain tiles, two bathrooms, and three bedrooms. Annie and Becca shared a room, Gigi and Roxy shared a room, and I was once again on my own. I would have been happy to stay with someone, but I knew they were probably afraid I'd talk my roommate's ear off!

I missed my mom a lot. I was truly on my own for the first time, and I didn't love it. While I did crave some independence like any eighteen-year-old, it was odd to experience so many big moments without her. She couldn't even enter the Paralympic Village, so the only time I saw her was at the barn.

That first day, I took a nap and focused on acclimating to the time, which was only about a two-hour difference from Training Camp in Texas. But it felt like so much more with all that had shifted. Having safely arrived at my destination with everything I needed in my one official bag, I finally could allow my body to relax. I couldn't *wait* for the next day to go see Rosie and ride. The anticipation was real!

LET THE GAMES BEGIN

We had arrived one week prior to the start of the Games to acclimate ourselves (and the horses, having left the United States before us, had had longer). There were shuttles that ran every thirty minutes from the Village to the venue, called "Bubble to Bubble" transportation. They could take us where we need to go without athletes having to go through security at every single point. Driving from the Paralympic Village to the venue, we traveled through a number of neighborhoods and were able to glimpse views of the "real" Brazil.

It was an approximately thirty-minute commute, but the traffic could make it forty-five.

The site of the equestrian events was an active military base. It was heavily guarded, and drills were run throughout the day, including the firing of weapons, which created drama with some of the horses.

Rosie, however, felt right at home. I was instantly thankful that she had grown used to such noise at our training barn in upstate New York, which had a gun range nearby. (We never doubted our horses' safety during the Games, knowing they were so well protected!)

It was at first strange to me that the barn walls were made of concrete. But as the week progressed and the weather got progressively hotter—with steam rising off the arena footing at times—practice became more and more difficult, and it became clear that the intense heat and humidity was buffered by the porous material, with the barns providing some relief to us all. I also learned that because concrete was more water-resistant than, say, wood, it was less likely to get moldy in the tropical environment. After years of working out of beautifully constructed show stables in the United States, there was something so efficient and even comfortable about the gray, unassuming stabling. The guards with guns and concrete blocks could have easily made me think of a prison, but nothing could be farther from the truth. Instead, I was at the Rio Paralympics, fulfilling a lifelong dream, and in that, there was a certain sense of freedom.

Our practice rides had to be short, sweet, and to the point, not only in recognition of the weather, but also so we didn't hit our peak before the competition. Rosie, unfortunately, began to show signs that she wasn't taking well to the changes of environment and travel. She began to cough during our schooling, throwing her head down as she did so, which yanked the reins from my one hand. Mom and Amy and I met with the Team Veterinarian, who, after performing an exam, suggested the mare likely had an allergy to the hay provided by the event organizers. We had no other option at the time but to continue with the feed we had, and despite the cough, Rosie was the only horse who had traveled with the Team who gained weight rather than lost a little during the transition (not an uncommon issue with international travel). She also seemed to be happy and engaged, albeit slightly lethargic in the heat. The veterinarian checked in daily to make sure she remained capable of proceeding with the competition, and I was even more careful of her well-being in our practice rides. If she had given any indication she couldn't perform, we would have pulled her immediately. But everyone agreed we should keep going.

My time at the barn in the runup to the Games was busy, and I looked forward to it, not only for my time in the saddle, but also for the chance to really get to know the venue—something extremely important because I only have one eye with vision and my depth perception is skewed.

Of course, the highlight was being able to see my mom every day. As I mentioned, she wasn't allowed in the Athlete's Village, which required a special day pass for visitors (and I hadn't manage to organize one for her—boy, is that still a bone of contention for us, to this day!). While I loved the Village and all its perks, I wasn't used to being on my own. Even in the athlete housing, where I was surrounded by my teammates, I felt more isolated than I was used to. My mom and I were a team, too, and this was the first time we had been separated.

The benefit for my mom was that, with me on my own in the Village, she had the freedom to spend time with the rest of my family who came to Rio de Janeiro to support me. She stayed with my dad, brothers, and grandparents at a hotel, and they had a lot of days to enjoy the beach and explore the neighboring area. It was special to know they were all there, even if I didn't get to see them as often as I would have liked.

It was a struggle for me to compartmentalize what was happening. I was only eighteen years old and separated from my family for the first time. I was used to relying on them for almost everything, which, to a certain degree, isn't different from many other kids my age, regardless of physical abilities. But instead of spending time with them and touring the wonderful country and culture of Brazil, I had to focus on my team and being part of something completely separate. I had to really focus on the competitive aspect and the bigger reasons why I was there while the people I loved were off having fun without me. This was a more difficult aspect to navigate without my mom right there next to me every day as a support system. In addition, I was learning to navigate the world without Journey. My service dog had become an important touchstone when I felt unbalanced mentally, as well as physically. I missed having him there beside me.

Rio was a pivotal moment in my life—yes, for obvious reasons, as it was the Paralympics. It was the most significant event in my athletic and advocacy career yet, and there was a lot of internalized pressure I was putting on myself so I would not let my team down. I was stress eating, and feeling isolated in an apartment with teammates who had become friends, but not family. I had so much riding on the event that it was almost overwhelming in scope. And now I was realizing the difficulty of doing it all without the support system I had relied so much on in all the years prior. But there was nothing I could do about it. I was still in the grasp of childhood.

It was at that moment that I faced adulthood and had to decide if I was turning forward or turning back.

Is anyone truly ready for what comes next? All the roads in my life, until that moment in Rio—every stroke, every catch ride, every good and bad thing—had all had one focus and one destination in mind. *The Paralympics.* Yes, I was there to help Team USA and my teammates bring home the gold, but I was also ready to show the world that anything and everything was possible with hard work and determination. I wanted to make a positive impact.

It was now time for me to put that goal into action, and it was terrifying and exhilarating at once.

Retrospect is funny. We are lucky if we regret nothing, but it is likely there are things we can identify as wishing we had done differently. Life has a way of teaching us lessons when we look back. All roads had led to Rio. Once I was there, it was both more and less than I expected. Physically, I'd been well prepared and was ready to ride. Emotionally, it was a different story.

The Jog, where horses are judged to be sound and fit to compete, went well, and every US horse passed inspection. I've always associated The Jog with what kicks off a show.

Finally, it was time.

One thing that was necessary for me at competitions was ring familiarization. I needed time to walk the arena and learn it prior to riding my test. With my limited eyesight and faulty depth perception, I had to get close and mentally map where my markers were. Kai Handt, our chef d'équipe, had confirmed with the show organizers I would have one-on-one time to do so in advance of my ride, either on foot or mounted on my horse.

The organizers kept pushing us off.

As we got closer and closer to competition day without a chance for me to be in the arena where we would compete, it became incredibly stressful. Ring familiarization was integral to my ride. Without it, I couldn't be the teammate I wanted or needed to be, as I would not be able to ride an accurate test. There was also a certain stability for me in ritual and knowing how things would move forward. The Jog and touring the ring were two things that were part of my "preparing to compete" process, and the delay in the latter was a hurdle that added to an increasing amount of internalized stress.

Finally, *on the same day and only an hour before we were to ride our test,* I was given permission to enter the ring on foot.

It was ninety degrees Fahrenheit, as I, dressed in my full dressage show gear, jacket and all, limped through the sand. The scenario was less than ideal for a number of reasons, but still, it was the only opportunity that had been offered, and I needed the process. So off I trod with my trainer Wes at my side to refine our points: the ends of the arena, the center, the corners. It was a lot of walking for me, but I wasn't about to complain. Looking for the bright side, Wes and I laughed and said, "What could be more 'Sydney' than this?"

I focused on what Rosie and I could do to have a great ride, but the walk out of the arena felt like miles. Wes shouted for my mobility scooter so I could rest a bit while he mounted Rosie and warmed her up for me. Now it was only a matter of time.

◇ ◇ ◇

I had expended more energy than I would have liked during the ring familiarization process. I was no stranger to heat or to exercise, but the timing was less than ideal. Still, I had no choice. In the blink of an eye, it was time for me to mount up. It all happened so fast. I went from walking the arena on foot, to sitting and watching Wes warm up Rosie, to getting on and preparing Rosie myself. *Boom, boom, boom.* The mare felt spot on, despite a little coughing as she cleared her throat of hay particles.

I was using a double rein with a "ladder" for my hand that helped me change my grip and contact with her mouth during the different gaits. The shortest length was for trotting; the medium length was for a working walk with some collection; and the longest length was for the free walk, when I asked Rosie to stretch over her back and neck. With a whip also in my hand, it was no small feat for me to adjust between these lengths. And I had all this to coordinate while somehow remembering my test and markers.

Dressage is a beautiful discipline and complicated to perform correctly, but when it is, it looks effortless. As a perfectionist, I aim for "correct," and I work hard so my disability does not get in the way of achieving that. My adaptive tools, like the ladder on my rein, help me, but switching between the rein lengths takes a leap of faith because I must leave my good hand open and do it by feel. All while keeping contact with the horse's mouth and moving forward—always forward.

I had to be smart with my timing, so the switching rein lengths didn't interfere with the test's required movements or the time allowed between them.

Before I knew it, it was my turn to ride down the centerline.

◇ ◇ ◇

Anyone who has competed in any way is probably familiar with the nerves that come with anticipation. While I live to compete, I still get excited and have butterflies.

There is a large difference between practicing in front of empty stands and riding a test in front of a large audience of people watching your every move. It adds a certain additional layer of pressure to perform. Plus, inside I was recognizing that this moment was what we had been working toward for years, and it was finally happening. My name was up on the jumbotron screen. The time was now, and I was so grateful to have such a wonderful horse to share it with me.

Wes took my reins and led me around the arena once before setting me up at the entryway so I could look down the centerline. I had a flashback to the World Equestrian Games when I'd almost run Wes over, but reminded myself that I had one minute to enter the arena and there was no need to rush. Rosie and I did a twenty-meter circle to set ourselves up well and then entered the arena, halting and saluting the judges.

That first centerline felt like we were floating on air.

My whole ride felt amazing at the time. It was a dream made real.

But when I rode out of the arena, the look on Wes's face said it all. I racked my brain for what might have gone wrong.

"Wes, what did I do?"

"Sydney, did that feel forward to you?"

"Yeah, it felt like I was flying!"

"Sydney, you were slower than molasses on a cold, winter day."

My whole positive self-image shattered.

My parents offered to show me the video they had taken of my ride so I could watch. I was shocked at how slowly Rosie and I had been going. In the ring, it had felt fast, like the world was racing by us. The dichotomy of how it felt versus how it looked made me question my own instincts in the show ring.

With all the confidence of an overachieving teenager, I had thought I was ready for the moment. But has anyone ever been truly ready for their first Paralympics?

I had never admitted to myself that I was experiencing nerves beyond the butterflies I was accustomed to when riding at shows. Afraid I wouldn't be able to conquer them, I buried them deeply and tried to hide them. I had ridden the test in fight-or-flight mode, tense and on the muscle, which clouded my perception of my ride and how Rosie was moving. Now, with the wisdom of age and experience, I can see my Paralympic debut for what it was—an almost overwhelming experience that I was mentally unprepared for, despite being physically capable. Burying my feelings and not having coping mechanisms in place to help me with my sense of isolation and internalized pressure had set me up for failure.

I could not have been more disappointed, not for myself but for the fact that I hadn't given my best to the Team. My movements were precise and my mare was feeling great, but my week of stress eating leading up to the ride, coupled with the long ring familiarization walk just before it, did not have me putting my best physical foot forward. And I truly believe my inability to understand or cope with my nerves prevented me from being my best for my horse, trainer, and team.

I walked away determined to start a new path. I knew I could have given a better performance. In athletics, there is always room for improvement. I promised to focus on self-development with nutrition, exercise, and a sport psychologist to help me with the mental component I clearly lacked.

When I was a little girl who loved riding horses, my dream to one day make the Olympic Team was born. When I was diagnosed with Wyburn-Mason and eventually found para dressage, my goal shifted to the Paralympics. I thought that riding in Rio would be the highlight of my life. That centerline in Brazil should have been the culmination of all my hard work. Instead, after my ride, I recognized that I still had a lot of work to do as an athlete and I had a much longer road ahead of me.

My original dream was that of a child who was unaware that personal progress never ends. Rio de Janeiro was the moment I rode forward into adulthood.

26
COMING DOWN

Despite my slow ride, I was still able to compete the second day, and my scores for that test were reasonable. My "grade," at the time, was the largest of all the classes, and I ended seventh out of twenty-two top riders from around the world, competing against many already decorated Paralympians. I even got a ribbon! Most importantly, I could hold my head high and be proud of my ability to come back and ride better, all while knowing that I needed to make some bigger changes to work my way up to the medal podium.

When what I had long deemed "the most pivotal moment in my life" was over, there was a gigantic endorphin release. Just as I'd experienced following my trip to the World Equestrian Games two years before, I erupted into tears when my rides were over, sobbing uncontrollably in my Paralympic Village apartment.

What now?

For the second time in my life, I felt like I didn't have a goal directly in front of me. Even after WEG and the "come down" I had experienced from that athletic high, I knew it would be full steam ahead for Rio. But now it was worse. I had been so focused on finding a way to represent the United States at the Rio 2016 Paralympics, I never gave serious thought to what would happen afterward.

I had begun to think about attending college, but I was worried about the cost. When I started to investigate my options, I was shocked to discover how little financial support was given to people with disabilities to attend, either in person or online. It was a harsh reality I'd never considered.

About time for a breakdown.

My mom took me for a grounding walk on the beach on our final night in Brazil, helping me get out of my head. I met up with the rest of my family and began the process of reconnecting with my support system.

I never stay in a funk for long, and the next day was a favorite of mine.

My team and our families were invited to visit Christ the Redeemer, the massive statue of Jesus Christ that sits on top of Corcovado Mountain in Rio de Janeiro. One means of reaching the statue is by tram through the surrounding jungle.

Of course, I had a clothing malfunction, which, as you know by now, is such a "me" thing to do. I wore basketball warm-up pants, something that I knew would be moisture-wicking and comfortable in the intense jungle air.

Bad idea. Terrible. Don't do it!

The pants were slick, and on the steep ascent to the top of the mountain, I repeatedly slid out of my hard plastic seat. I held on for dear life, not wanting to plummet to my death.

The ride itself was beautiful, with astounding views, and when I could find some stability, whenever we went through sections of jungle, my mom and I would search for monkeys in the lush foliage.

I noticed a boy with limb differences also riding the tram. He and I chatted a bit, finding a way to communicate, despite the language difference (he spoke Portuguese), and I told him my team and I were there for the Paralympics. Later I wondered if one day he would remember meeting someone different, like him, who was doing something amazing. Would that give him some confidence or motivation to reach a goal of his own one day? It was a brief encounter that sticks with me, and I hope he has found happiness in life.

The more people I can reach and help to understand my syndrome, the challenges I face, and my sport, the more they can inform others and share in this positive and expanding web of education. Together, we can spread awareness that *disability* doesn't mean *incapable*. Everyone has something that makes them different, whether it is visible or not.

I'm the only person alive with Wyburn-Mason syndrome. As much as it hurts to admit, at one point, I thought it would be easier if I shaved my head while I was going through treatments that caused bald spots, as then people would simply assume I had cancer. Luckily, my mom was wise and advised against such drastic measures. But having a rare diagnosis meant I wasn't able to meet others with the same condition, and people off the street didn't understand me or what I was going through. It's a unique experience, growing up with a rare medical condition, explaining it over and over. In many ways, it means I'm isolated, always. That feeling has made me very aware of how I treat other people and extremely grateful for the connections I do have.

◇ ◇ ◇

Once I survived the treacherous tram to Christ the Redeemer, my booty sliding every which way, my team and our families were piled on top of each other at the peak of the mountain, with five wheelchairs and suffocating crowds of people. There was a huge line for the elevator to reach the statue's feet, so only a few team members could use it. I opted to instead walk up the stairs with the support of my family, with someone carrying my wheelchair so I could use it when we reached the top.

The view was breathtaking, a full three-hundred-sixty-degree panorama of the city, ocean, mountains, and jungle. The drop over the side was treacherous, and the crowd became claustrophobic. It was exhilarating! My family was terrified that I would be my clumsy self and topple over the edge. Luckily, we managed to enjoy the view, and nobody careened off the edge.

My mom flew back from Brazil with me, on the plane with the rest of the athletes. She'd never been in such a small space with so many people with disabilities, so it was eye-opening for her. She had to grow accepting of the sight of a gold medalist in muscle spasm, which happened with a few of our athletes periodically throughout the flight. For us, that kind of thing was the norm.

After a brief return to Texas with the Team, we flew immediately back to New York to pick up our car, and then drove on to Michigan. It was time to get back to our "normal" routine. I was excited to be home, but no one was more excited than Journey. When we picked him up in Michigan, his reaction was priceless. He was energetic by nature, but he virtually burst when he saw us coming, launching himself toward me. I felt the same exact way. He was my best friend and my only source of freedom when I wasn't on a horse.

THE WHITE HOUSE

27

About three weeks after the close of the Paralympics, my mom received an official email, inviting us (along with my whole team and other Team USA athletes) to visit the White House.

You read that correctly. As if I was going to turn that down!

I was in disbelief. Only six years before, I was looking for a purpose. Now, I was celebrating with world leaders!

Journey and I shared a room with my teammate Annie in the hotel where all the Olympians and Paralympians were staying together. My mom stayed with Annie's mom for the weekend, so she would get to spend the weekend with a friend, too. Shuttles were provided to transport us between the hotel and the White House. As we waited out front with masses of athletes, one bus was filling, and an organizer called out that there was one available spot. Being me, I jumped at the chance to get on with a bunch of strangers and make new friends. I didn't even think twice about leaving my teammatesbehind to catch up on another shuttle! I had no idea, though, that Journey and I had jumped on the bus full of Olympic swimmers and gymnasts and that I would be sitting near gymnast Gabby Douglas! I was starstruck and thought to myself, *My team is going to hate that I got to meet all these people by leaving them to catch the next shuttle!*

I was the only Paralympian on that bus; I introduced myself to *everyone.*

Even though the hotel was near the White House, the ride took about forty-five minutes in the surrounding DC traffic, and I chatted with my neighbors, as we all joked and had a lot of fun. Everyone was cool and welcoming. Journey, as usual, was very popular.

Mom and the rest of my team met me at the White House grounds, where we all went through security, received a guided tour, and then enjoyed exploring the public areas of the property. Eventually, we were ushered into the Press Room to wait for President Obama. We all lined up, Olympians and Paralympians alike, to shake the hand of the President of the United States, the First Lady, and Vice-President Biden, who came through and greeted us all.

In honor of the Paralympics, I had dyed my hair blue at the roots with red ends. I felt it was a very patriotic statement! When President Obama shook my hand, he said, "Hey, I like your hair."

I blushed. My hair was Obama-approved!

When the First Lady came through next, I had to ask her, "Do you remember me?"

Michelle Obama replied graciously, "Of course I remember you!" And as if that wasn't amazing enough, she gave me another hug! I've officially now been hugged twice by a First Lady.

Vice-President Biden shook my hand and kissed both my cheeks before reaching down to pet Journey, who basked in the glory.

 BEYOND EXPECTATIONS

Don't mind me fan-girling!

President Obama gave a little speech to our group, and Gabby Douglas and a few others were also asked to make remarks. Then we were shuttled back to the hotel to primp for the gala and awards event to be held that evening in celebration of all the 2016 athletes.

At the party, it was amazing to catch up with the teammates and coaches I hadn't seen since we'd left Texas after returning from Rio. Everyone looked completely different dressed up in their fancy clothing, as opposed to how I remembered them in their approved Paralymmpic athletic gear. Those athletes whose embossed rings had been completed already wore them proudly. (I was still waiting for mine.)

President Obama had also invited the eighteen African-Americans who competed for the United States in the 1936 Olympics in Nazi Germany, and their family members. They had returned home to a segregated country and were not invited to visit the White House as was custom by then-President Franklin Roosevelt. I felt honored to be present as they were recognized the way they deserved, decades later.

I danced the night away, although unfortunately, I didn't have as much luck with the President of the United States on the dance floor as I had with the President of Azerbaijan! Still, it was wonderful to be a Paralympian, celebrated alongside our Olympic counterparts and treated equally.

A NOT-SO-GENTLE REMINDER OF MY MORTALITY

It would be this stroke, out of all of them, that I would remember the most vividly.

After months that were a whirlwind of excitement and successes, I began the work of taking what I had learned in Rio and setting my sights forward with the new goal of qualifying for the next Paralympics in Tokyo (2020).

But with the highs came the lows. Each of the four strokes I'd had further limited my abilities and likely took years off my life. They were an unwelcome reminder of the ever-present timebomb lurking behind my right eye, deep inside my brain.

My fifth stroke came while my mom was at home in Michigan, spending time with my dad and brothers. Grammy was staying with me in New York so I could continue training.

That day I had a very difficult time riding Wentworth in my lesson. Even during "downtime," I'm always working with my horses and focusing on improvement. But this was the hardest ride I'd had to date. My body felt sore and disconnected, and that whole week I had been experiencing migraine headaches. Nothing was clicking, and I was incredibly frustrated.

In some ways, it's easier to connect the patterns, looking back on all my strokes. Before each one, I would experience clumsiness or migraine headaches. These should have been subtle warning signs, but they were easily ignored as symptoms of stress or me just being silly old me.

On this day, I went home after my difficult ride and went immediately to bed, where I slept hard through the night. When I woke up the next morning, I got out of bed, took my first step with my stronger right leg, then moved to take another step with my left leg. It wasn't there. I couldn't feel it, nor would it move when I wanted to take a step forward. So I set off for the living room, stepping with my right leg and dragging my left, calling out to my grandmother. When I reached her, we called my mom at once.

Thank goodness for a non-alarmist mom. I tend to panic, and my mom counters that with abnormal calm to try and keep me from freaking out.

"Oh, Syd," Mom said. "You probably just had a hard ride yesterday. Take a day off and if it's not back by tomorrow, we'll go to the doctor."

I knew it was bigger than that.

"But I can't tell my leg to do anything!" I insisted.

"That's why you shouldn't ride today. If rest helps, we'll know it was just sore from a hard ride."

I step-dragged myself back to bed, still with an ever-present migraine, and fell back asleep.

I woke up again the next day, ready to reassess. I called my mom again.

"Mom, you know the hospital is the last place I want to be…"

"Okay, Syd. If there has been no improvement, it's time to go see the doctors."

I really didn't want to go. It was the same every time. Doctors who had zero experience with Wyburn-Mason syndrome because they'd, at most, only read about it. Then, all my physical symptoms got blamed on the AVMs, regardless on what might be the real cause. It was never a quick visit to the emergency room. Instead, it would be a full medical history and CT scans, then days at the hospital, "just in case."

I know this sounds like I don't appreciate everything doctors have done for me. That is not the case. I'm grateful that I'm still alive, I'm riding horses, and I'm pursuing my dreams. But after years of medical treatments and the resulting side effects, I just wanted to be able to ride horses and live my life.

While I knew my symptoms were serious, I procrastinated as much as possible, dreading the whole ordeal. Grammy and I didn't make it to the hospital until late afternoon.

◇ ◇ ◇

By the time we reached the hospital in Poughkeepsie, my migraine was bad enough to cause a panic attack. I started crying and hyperventilated so badly my body stopped sending blood to my right arm. Suddenly, I couldn't feel my "good" arm, which caused me to panic further, thinking I was running out of working limbs. I tried to pick up my phone, but my fingers wouldn't grasp it, sending me into a downward spiral.

Upon arrival at the ER, doctors requested an MRI and CT scan at once. My anger switch flipped on, and I refused, saying I didn't want to take out my nose piercing for no reason. Inevitably (and sensibly) I gave in.

There was a rub, though: the doctors didn't know how to read my scans without any experience with AVMs. They surmised, "You probably had another stroke, and that would explain your symptoms."

Yes, now I couldn't walk unless I moved my right leg and dragged my left leg behind me—incredibly dangerous, given the rest of my physical challenges. The stroke had happened at home, and the damage was already done, but once again I had to remain hospitalized as I dealt with excruciating pain from the migraine.

My mom flew in from Michigan to whip the hospital into shape, support me, and handle the insurance company.

In my second week in the hospital, I went to wash my left side in the shower, but realized I couldn't feel the water running down that part of my body. Until that point, I had altered perception on my left, but I could feel things—it was just different from the right side of my body. That shower was the first time I felt nothing at all. The heat from the steam, the droplets of water, none of it registered on one side of my body. I could see it there, but it was like one half of my body didn't exist anymore to my brain. It was completely blank.

Water was always a catalyst of sorts for me. After my first stroke at eleven years old, I'd noticed the differences in my perception more after swimming. It felt like my right side was in water, but there was a bubble around the left, like it wasn't getting wet. I could see it in the water, but it didn't *feel* like it was. Talk about messing with my mind. Now, after my fifth stroke, it made sense to me that I would recognize the full extent of the damage while I was in the shower.

It was now like there was a line, dividing my body in two.

Thankfully, the doctors were just as alarmed by my lack of feeling, and my mom had already gotten me accepted into in-patient rehabilitation in the hopes I wouldn't lose any more mobility. It was a more intensive program for recovery than the hospital would supply on its own. I'd proven I could fight back from a stroke before, and I was determined to do so again. The doctors approved my transfer to the rehab facility in West Haverstraw, New York, more than three hours south of where we were living. Journey was allowed to stay with me there, after some advocacy on our parts.

Once again, I was the youngest and coolest person in the Stroke Unit. I made friends with a lot of my older neighbors in the wing, and it made it easier for me to be away from my friends and family. My mom stayed as much as she could, traveling back and forth from our rental home.

◇　◇　◇

The nursing staff at the rehab facility was amazing. Physical therapy, occupational therapy, and recreational therapy were all part of my treatment program. I loved recreational therapy; my therapist Eileen and her student Mallory made it fun. Mallory had amazing energy and embraced alternative fashion, like me, so we really clicked. Through her I met two younger guys who were inpatients also—she encouraged me to roll down to their wings and introduce myself. They were new to their injuries and altered bodies, so I wanted to be a positive influence as they came to understand what would be a new lifestyle. Plus, I loved having someone around who was my age! Having friends and a purpose gave me some light in a lonely time where I was trying now for the *third* time to relearn how to walk.

I spent hours on a treadmill with a bungee harness that helped take the pressure off my legs. I felt like I imagined it must feel walking in space. My right leg did well, but an assistant had to pick up my left leg and move it through each stride to begin to retrain the muscles to refire. It was work in the pool that I found made the biggest difference in regaining my mobility.

There was water, once again having a huge impact.

While I was rehabbing, I struggled to keep up with my college courses online. I had found and applied to receive a full scholarship at DeVry University through the Athlete Career Education Program (through the United States Olympic and Paralympic Committee), and two weeks later had been accepted. I was so grateful that my being a part of para dressage had given me opportunities others didn't have access to. Even though it was hard to stay focused, the classes and homework did help me stay busy and less focused on the time I was spending away from the horses and my riding.

That fifth stroke was a serious setback.

You may remember that I was born on Thanksgiving in 1997. Well, in 2016, my birthday fell once again on Thanksgiving Day, which I had to spend in the rehabilitation center. My whole family came to visit me, and we ordered Chinese takeout and ate it all together in my little room. I was forced to watch the football game (ugh), but I was so elated to have them there with me, it was worth it! Nothing helped the migraine pain that still wouldn't go away—not even Percocet and Valium—but having my family there with me to celebrate my nineteenth birthday and Thanksgiving did help ease the pain in my soul.

I was in in-patient rehab until late December, after spending a full two months working on recovery. I don't remember a lot of the Christmas holiday that year; it was a blur due to pain and medication. But I was just happy to be home with my family.

The first time I had the chance, I returned to the barn. Wes had me sit on a young horse named Fritz. That moment was the happiest I'd felt in months. I could breathe again. My fifth stroke was such a huge contraction from the highest of highs in Brazil. But if I could still have horses in my life, I'd be okay.

When I was finally able to go back to my home barn full time, after months of recovery and rehabilitation, I was physically changed. I now rolled down the barn aisleway in my wheelchair, rather than walking like I used to. But horses were the constant in my life. Once I stuck my feet in the stirrups again, it felt like coming home. All my recent struggles faded away. All the mattered was the time on the horse. Wyburn-Mason couldn't take that away from me.

Despite the many goals I've achieved and adventures I've had so far in my life, I'm nowhere near done. Having Wyburn-Mason syndrome, and being one of the very few people alive with it, could have meant self-isolation, depression, and allowing myself to be treated like I'm a victim. I am an unusual case: I was able-bodied until I was eight years old, walked the line between both worlds for a few years, and am now disabled after multiple strokes. I know what it is like to be built differently. Despite the bad days and the many struggles I've overcome (and am still overcoming), the journey has strengthened me as a human being.

My family and close friends have always held me accountable and treated me like an individual rather filing me under the label of "disabled" or coddling me, trying to protect me from the world. I've tried and failed at things. I've tried and succeeded. At times I've been treated as "less than," and I have chosen not to accept the limitations others may have tried to place on me, whether it was in the school system, in barns where owners didn't want me to ride their horses because of liability, or on the streets of the cities I have been lucky to visit.

I am not less than. *You* are not less than. I will be the one to lift you up and show you that it *can* be done. Life and goals and getting out of bed every day is hard work, yes. Absolutely. Some days you may think you can't move forward because you are built differently—whether in a way that is visible to others or not. Making life work can be daunting.

Disabled isn't a dirty word.

We're all differently abled to handle the challenges life presents. We're all imperfectly human. I'm living, breathing, fighting proof that there is a champion in all of us, if only we put forth the hard work, day in and day out, and remember to surround ourselves with those who believe in us.

Every one of us can rise beyond expectations.

ACKNOWLEDGMENTS

To everyone who ever helped host a fundraiser or donated to make this quest possible, thank you for believing in me when I needed it most. Your donations made it possible for me to ride into the person I am today. Your kindness is appreciated from the bottom of my heart and my entire sense of being! I hope you know that you're riding down centerline with me every step of the way.

Mom and Dad, thank you for sacrificing more than ten years of your marriage to a long-distance relationship so I could pursue my elite-level goals. That sacrifice is something that not many marriages could survive, but your love is so strong that no matter how many miles were (or are) between us, we were always right there with one another.

Dad, thank you for always being so confident in my abilities. I don't know where my rides would be without your encouragement, support, and overall positive vibe. Our pre- or post-show calls mean more to me than I think you'll ever know. You have a way of making me feel like the most powerful version of myself wherever you are in the world. You are one-of-a-kind, and I am lucky to call you Dad! Thank you for all your sacrifices and hard work, and for being the glue that holds our family together.

Mom, thank you for selflessly dedicating so much of your life to my goal of wanting to make a positive difference in the world. Your unwavering belief in me and my ability to persist no matter the situation has truly molded me into the woman I am today and has made this book a possibility.

Alex and Simon, thank you for your sacrifice and for putting up with having a long-distance sister and mother for so many years. You are so strong, independent, and grown up, it blows my mind! I'm so proud of both of you—Simon, for your incredible academic achievements, and Alex, for the beautiful family you have created with your wife Madi and son Jaxson, as well as your own incredible academic achievements. The men you are both growing up to be amaze me daily. You both challenge me to be the best version of myself in the best way—and in a way that only siblings can! (No, that is *not* permission to gang up on me more to "challenge me.")

And of course, to my grandparents, both here with me and in heaven looking over me every day. Pop Pop, I will never forget our many drives to and from high school, to see Nanny at her retirement community, and of course our culinary adventures when you'd give me a hard time about not having more eclectic tastes! Grammy, thank you for your selflessness and for always being there with a warm hug whether it's in person or virtually. Your positive attitude and kindness to everyone you cross paths with is something that this world needs more than 100 times over, and I am so blessed to call you my "Gram" and "Grammy Groom!"

New Grammy Nanny, you were such a shining light in this world, there isn't a day that goes by that I don't miss our conversations or look back fondly on our drives through the California mountainsides, singing our favorite song that annoyed everyone else in the car (that we just kept singing until they joined in!). You didn't know much about horses, nor were they your passion, but for years you would come with us and work long horse show days as one half of my dedicated Grammy Grooms team. Those years were my absolute favorites. To this day it is still weird showing in Wellington, Florida, without you there with us. I wish you could be here to read this book, but I know that you're here with me every day and just want you to know that your presence and love were a highlight of my life. Without you, I don't know where I would be. Grandpa, I remember when I was young being kind of intimidated when talking with you. I think I never wanted to say the wrong thing, and I struggled to keep eye contact. Imagine that—*me* being intimidated when talking with someone! I am very happy I got over that, because as I have grown up our deep conversations about the state of the world, life, and my life's trajectory are some of my most cherished memories—those, and all our fun times in Maine on the Enkidu sailboat and the "Marjorie Anne," going to Otter Island and traversing the wilds of all around.

For years I wondered how I could ever repay the countless sacrifices you have all made along the path of my pursuit of greatness and my desire to make a positive impact on the world around us. My hope is that this book shows just how grateful I am for all our memories, and for beinglucky enough to be born into such a one-of-a-kind family that never gave up on me or my goals, even when the going got tough or when doctors were telling you there was no other option. Every one of you always fought for me to have a life just as full of love and passion as any able-bodied person. You never made me think I was ridiculous for setting such big goals, and that is something that everyone should get to experience within their lifetime. My ability to strive for this success in every facet of my life and my positive attitude is all thanks to every one of you—your positive attitudes, your senses of humor, and your critical-yet-kind perspectives. You have all formed me into the woman that I am today, and for that I'm forever grateful.

Last but never least, Jonathan Wentz, my friend, mentor, and confidante—of course this book is dedicated to you, too! I want to thank you for putting all this into motion at the moment we first met back in 2010 while you were representing the United States at the World Equestrian Games in Kentucky. You were the catalyst who set this fire within my soul and truly showed me that it was okay to learn how to accept my body through the discovery of the sport of para dressage. You and I should be writing books and making teams alongside one another! It breaks my heart that you aren't here to be part of this and to be right by my side. I was lucky enough to get to know you and look up to you, even for only a short time. Just know that all my rides, every step of the way, you are always in my heart, propelling me toward the next goal and *forward*.

Jonathan, you ride on with me!

INDEX

Plate numbers, in *italics*, correspond to numbered images
in the photo insert pages.